Learning with Online and Mobile Technologies

Learning with Online and Mobile Technologies

A Student Survival Guide

JANET MACDONALD
and
LINDA CREANOR

GOWER

Published by
Gower Publishing Limited
Wey Court East
Union Road
Farnham
Surrey
GU9 7PT
England

Gower Publishing Company
Suite 420
101 Cherry Street
Burlington
VT 05401-4405
USA

www.gowerpublishing.com

Janet MacDonald and Linda Creanor have asserted their moral right under the Copyright, Designs and Patents Act, 1988, to be identified as the authors of this work.

British Library Cataloguing in Publication Data
MacDonald, Janet, 1950-
 Learning with online and mobile technologies : a student
 survival guide.
 1. Education, Higher--Computer-assisted instruction.
 2. Internet in higher education. 3. Mobile communication
 systems in education. 4. Computers and college students.
 5. Distance education.
 I. Title II. Creanor, Linda.
 378.1'734-dc22

ISBN: 978-0-566-08930-5 (pbk)
      978-0-566-08931-2 (ebk)

Library of Congress Cataloging-in-Publication Data
MacDonald, Janet, 1950-
 Learning with online and mobile technologies : a student survival guide / by
Janet MacDonald and Linda Creanor.
     p. cm.
 ISBN 978-0-566-08930-5 (pbk.) -- ISBN 978-0-566-08931-2 (ebook)
 1. Computer-assisted instruction. 2. Mobile communication systems. 3.
College student orientation. I. Creanor, Linda. II. Title.
 LB1028.5.M1245 2010
 378.1'734--dc22

                                                              2009052392

Mixed Sources
Product group from well-managed
forests and other controlled sources
www.fsc.org Cert no. SA-COC-1565
© 1996 Forest Stewardship Council
FSC

Printed and bound in Great Britain by
MPG Books Group, UK

Contents

List of Figures

Acknowledgements

The material in this book draws on research and practice that we have been involved in over the last few years. The quotes from students are based on what has been said or written to us over this period in the various educational settings where we have worked and in our research of the use of learning technology by staff and students.

We would like to thank colleagues and students in our respective institutions who contributed moral support or helpful comments. Some individuals made a particular contribution and deserve a mention. Our thanks to those students from the Open University in Scotland's online peer support programme who contributed their experiences of study. Amongst staff at the OU we are thankful to the Library for their PROMPT checklist for evaluating resources; to Robin Harding for his musings on approaches to paraphrasing in Science; and to Phil Butcher for an example of a formative online quiz. At Glasgow Caledonian University we are grateful to Douglas Chalmers for providing the wiki screenshot; Kathy Trinder and the CUThere team for the Second Life example; the students who shared with us their experiences of learning with technology; and colleagues in the Caledonian Academy for their encouragement and good advice.

We are grateful to our families for their support, particularly Murdo and Helen in proofreading and producing some of the examples, as well as building the book website, and Kenneth in drawing the splendid illustrations.

Writing this book has been a collaborative project in which we have learnt much from each other. We come from different university backgrounds, one campus based and one open and distance, and the collaborative writing process has been both surprising and rewarding, in learning about the overlaps in interest and also where our experiences and those of our students differ. We hope that this book reflects that richness and variety.

Reviews for *Learning with Online and Mobile Technologies*

'A timely, helpful and easily readable book for any student wanting to get the most from the Internet and their mobile device.'

Niall Sclater Director of Learning Innovation, Open University

'This book is fantastic, especially for a student just coming to University. It pulls together nicely what university learning is all about and gives you that essential point of reference for all those tasks that seem daunting such as taking notes in a lecture or beginning to resource an assignment – I wish I had something like this when I first arrived.'

Sara Milne, Vice President Student Development, Students Association, Glasgow Caledonian University

'Whizz or dumbo with technology? Whatever... everyone needs to know the best ways of learning on the Web and on the move! It's all here.'

Professor Gilly Salmon, Professor of E-learning & Learning Technologies, Head of the Beyond Distance Research Alliance at the University of Leicester

'Chapter 5 provides an overview of and key advice on making sense of course materials and the different approaches to learning. The 'good practice guidelines' give clear and concise ideas to help students to identify the various tools that will help them in their studies, from ways of taking notes and tips on reading to practical ideas for file storage and innovative suggestions for keeping a learning diary. The text is easy to read, with boxes giving summaries of research on learning for those who are interested in finding out more about theories of learning, useful quotes from students describing tools that have helped them in their studies, and web links to free tools such as mind mapping software and file sharing websites.'

Rachel Leslie, student

'Chapter 3 offers really useful advice about the equipment you might need and where you might access this, including advice on planning for any difficulties that you might encounter. It gives advice on planning your studies to make best use of your time and the technologies you will be using and offers a list of resources for developing the skills required.'

Maria McCrea, educational adviser

'The chapter "Communicating and Community" really shows how varied and useful online communication tools are; it clearly explains how well they can be applied to learning and tutor and peer support when studying.'

Clare Fenton, student

'I found the text clearly and logically presented which helped to make it both engaging and interesting. The authors clearly understand my needs as a student. The advice given by the book was relevant and easily applicable to real-life situations. I will be able to use the helpful hints and tips to improve my work straightaway.'

Jonathan Hickie, student

'Chapter 7, "Communicating and Community: a survival guide" proves to be just that, by clearly and thoughtfully steering you through the various stages, potential pitfalls and good practice about communication generally as well as how to use various online communication tools when studying. As a tutor, I regularly use online communication tools and I'll refer students to this chapter to help allay their fears, build on their existing communication skills and develop their expertise in effectively using these tools for study purposes.'

Ebony Quinn, tutor

'This is an excellent survival guide which is relevant to all students irrespective of their experience of studying with online and mobile technologies. I like the way the technologies are clearly related to their uses outlined in the core areas of course content, communications, research and presentation. The clear accessible language plus the useful tips, summaries and illustrations all contribute to making online study a worthwhile experience rather than a technological minefield. I wish it had been available when I recently participated in an online group research project – it would have greatly improved our communication skills!'

Moira Harris, student

'The chapter on writing and presenting gives valuable information on the tools that can be used for academic writing online. The section on which tools can be used, for example, word processing, spreadsheets and presentation software are particularly useful and provide students with best practice hints and tips.'

Carla Munro, student

'The information on the use of new technologies like wikis is really helpful. Wikis are an easy, effective and efficient way for our entire class to learn together and share information. I especially like the fact that our class wiki can be *continuously updated, and that everyone can contribute. It is perfect for this honours year when we need all the help we can get.'*

Lyndsay Macrae, student

'I liked the communication chapter which explains about online discussion boards as it very much reflects my own experience. At first it is easy to be sceptical, however online discussion is beneficial as an alternative to classroom seminars. I definitely enjoyed the experience and I feel as if it made me focus more on preparing a really good answer because I was effectively posting to an audience.'

Student

'This book would have been very helpful to me in preparing for using online discussion boards as I was unsure about them at first. However, as the weeks went on I began to enjoy taking part. I thought it was a good basis to have a discussion as you did not need to respond to peoples comments immediately, you could take time to think of a suitable response. This meant things were rarely said that people did not mean, also it gave you time to look for sources to back up your argument.'

Student

'I agree with what this book says about learning online, especially on communicating with other students. During my course I always read extensively prior to posting anything on the discussion board thus felt better prepared to respond to the other group members' comments. I think I used my time well and more effectively than I would in a seminar where I often tend to wander from the subject at hand, then have to backtrack later and learn what I need for exams.'

Student

1 Introduction

I started a new course last year and was wondering how I was going to cope with it all, trying to find the best way to learn all this stuff and terrified when I had to write my first assignment. To me it's just learning, and the fact that it's online as opposed to in a classroom is irrelevant. I suppose I hadn't really given much thought to the technology, I hadn't realised how much it could help.

1

Online and mobile technologies have opened up exciting new possibilities for study in higher education, with important opportunities for students. Technology has become a necessary and everyday part of studying. This book starts with effective practice in learning, and shows how technology can support that good practice. We aim to show you the many ways in which online and mobile technologies can be used for study and give you some guidance on how best to use them for learning in higher education, whether that is at college or university, or within your workplace.

WHO SHOULD READ THIS BOOK

While some students follow a course which is completely online, most students make use of online and mobile technologies alongside their attendance at classes or tutorials, the use of text books, or the discussion of project work over a cup of coffee in classroom or corridor. Recently, the term 'blended learning' has been used to describe learning which takes place online as well as in face-to-face sessions, and that is probably the most common situation for the majority of students.

Some students attend a campus while others will study part time and some study at a distance. In addition to school leavers that includes mature or part-time students, or those undertaking continuous professional development or work-based training. We intend this book to cater to all these students, whatever their context. We also welcome members of staff as readers who may wish to update their knowledge of the use of technologies in academic study. Whatever background you are starting from, you will have strengths on which you can draw, whether you have studied previously or gained useful experience from everyday life, where the Internet is widely in use.

A note about rapid change

We all know that technology changes rapidly. What is in vogue today may not be popular in a year, or even in six months time, so we have concentrated on basing the advice in this book on what is already known about good practice in effective learning. We are reasonably confident that these principles should remain current even though the technologies may change, and we hope this should provide a good foundation for learning with technologies which have yet to appear.

WHY WE HAVE WRITTEN THIS BOOK

We have written this book because online and mobile technologies are now widespread in higher education and as a student it is important for you to know how to use them to support your learning. Technology plays a central role in most universities and colleges. Computers are widely in use by students and staff to access online resources and communicate with each other, and mobile technologies are also increasingly used for education, providing additional flexibility in study routines and an alternative way to access the Internet or communicate with fellow students.

Strengths of digital everything

One of the great strengths of online and mobile technologies is their potential to operate together for communicating, saving, editing or sharing information and resources. For example, you might use your mobile phone to record an audio clip, upload it to your computer and then attach it to an email to send to a friend, or perhaps post it on a social networking site to introduce yourself to fellow students. You might access a website from your computer, summarise the content in a word-processed document, incorporate it into your next assignment, and finally add photos you have uploaded from your camera. You then email the assignment to your tutor, and save the file to return to for revision purposes. Or you might download a podcast from your course website and then transfer it to an MP3 player, to play while you are travelling or exercising. Once information is in digital form it can be saved, edited, merged, or shared in many different ways.

These technologies also allow you to work at your own pace whether you need flexibility in time or in location, of particular importance if you are a part-time student. Technology might be used for delivery of content in the form of downloadable handouts, or whole course units, or podcasts on topics of interest. It can also be used for communication and dialogue, offering an alternative approach to learning in a conventional classroom.

Lifelong learning and you

We believe that the issues and good practice which we describe in this book will be relevant to you, not only in your course but in whatever learning situation you subsequently find yourself. People have always undertaken learning in a wide variety of circumstances in every day life, whether to find out how to bring up children, or to learn how to cope with new situations at work, or to contribute to the community. The term 'lifelong learning' has become a by-word today, and you will need to keep learning throughout life, whether or not you attend a formal course.

The use of technology has become an integral part of lifelong learning, and so have new approaches to learning which are particularly relevant to study through life. For example, the flexibility and greater choices possible when using online technologies for study mean that you will learn to be much more disciplined about time management than you would if you were only attending regular classes. You will develop independence and self-direction, so that when faced with a bewildering choice of web-based resources you are confident about how much to read, and when to stop. You will also need self-motivation if you are less dependent on class contact time to keep on top of study routines. As an effective lifelong learner you will learn not only the appropriate use of technologies, but also develop a self-disciplined and critical approach to study. So we believe that many of the approaches, skills and techniques which we talk about in this book will be of value to you not only in your formal course of study, but also in any other learning you might wish to undertake in future. In an increasingly competitive job market this will also be attractive to prospective employers.

Technology use is not an end in itself

Finally it is worth remembering that while technology can facilitate lifelong learning, it does not guarantee that learning will take place. The opportunities to develop independent or collaborative learning through a course can be supported by technology, but this will not work effectively unless the course is designed to support learning in new ways. While the extensive resources on the web provide knowledge and information which can easily be kept up to date, they are of little use to those who do not have reliable access to the Internet, and can instead deepen the divide between those with access and those without. On the other hand, communication technologies can also bridge divides by allowing contact between fellow students regardless of geography, disability or family responsibilities.

WHAT THIS BOOK CONTAINS

We hope you will read this book from cover to cover, but being realistic we recognise that some chapters will be of more interest and relevance to some of you than others. Here is an overview to give you a flavour of what each part of the book contains. What you read will depend on who you are, and what you know already. For these reasons, the chapters in this book will encourage you to draw on relevant previous experience in focusing on the process of learning: when considering why technologies will help, how and when.

We thought this book should draw on students' experiences, so that readers have a real sense that others have 'been there' and not only survived but derived positive benefit from using digital technologies for study. Their experiences underline the fact that studying using online or mobile technologies does not rely simply on technological skills, but draws on a range of abilities. In Chapter 2, *Student voices* we describe students with a diversity of backgrounds who came to be using technologies at colleges and universities. You may recognise experiences similar to your own, or perhaps gain confidence from seeing that you are not alone in thinking that you lack the necessary abilities.

You may wonder whether any study that requires online access will fit into your life, or perhaps feel anxious about basic skills in using a computer. For those who are starting from scratch and plan to get up to speed sufficiently with technology to feel comfortable about attending college or university at all, Chapter 3, *Practicalities* gives you some basic advice on the bottom line: the skills and equipment you need to get organised.

The rest of the book covers the processes of study in four closely related areas, as we illustrate in this diagram. In each of the four areas the chapters are written in pairs: describing first how online and mobile technologies are used in higher education, and then secondly providing a survival guide to good practice. The paragraphs which follow tell you more about the contents of each chapter.

If you start study in a new subject area or have been out of full-time education for some time then you may feel anxious when confronted

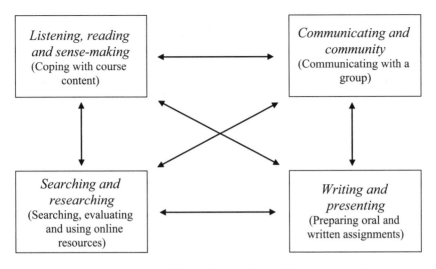

Figure 1.1   Studying with online and mobile technologies

with knowledge which is new and unfamiliar, in a language which can be rather alienating. Chapters 4 and 5 discuss *Listening, reading and sense-making,* in other words the processes which you go through when you are grappling with course content. We describe a range of ways in which this may take place using technologies and offer guidelines on good practice using various tools.

You may be a regular email user and wondering how communicating with fellow students could help your study. Perhaps you are nervous at the thought of studying off campus, effectively on your own. Chapters 6 and 7 discuss *Communicating and community,* describing the ways in which you communicate with a group, together with guidelines on communicating appropriately using a variety of tools.

You may be good at browsing the web and perhaps you are wondering what resources are appropriate for study, or whether you should be using them at all. Or maybe you are studying in English although that is not your first language and concerned about good practice in using online resources well. Chapters 8 and 9 cover the process of *Searching and researching,* by describing ways in which searching for online resources can contribute to your study. They give you some good practice guidelines for recognising useful sources and approaching the task of effective paraphrasing, summarising and referencing, while avoiding plagiarism.

You may have word-processed an important letter, or reports for work, or perhaps a column for the community newsletter, but you might wonder how relevant this experience is for writing in higher education. Chapters 10 and 11 discuss *Writing and presenting,* illustrating ways in which various tools are used for preparing oral and written assignments and offering guidelines for good practice.

Finally we recognise that many of the specialist terms in this book may be new, particularly if you start in the middle rather at the beginning, so we have provided a glossary which explains those terms we have used. Throughout the book are a large number of examples with further resources which you may wish to explore. We have collated all the links to these resources and presented them at the end of the book, and you will also find them on our book website, where you are welcome to add to them, or perhaps update links which no longer work. The website is to be found at: http://sites.google.com/site/learnonlinegroup/.

FINAL COMMENTS

Whether you are already confident with a variety of online or mobile technologies or are completely confused by anything digital, this book will provide a practical introduction to the key aspects of using technology effectively for learning and help you to make the most of the opportunities which online media and mobile devices can provide. The next chapter continues the theme of who should read this book by describing stories from students who come from a wide variety of backgrounds, with a range of experiences of study using technology.

2 Student Voices

Students in higher education come in all shapes and sizes, indeed we would find it hard to predict your own background and interests. You might be a school leaver or a mature student, in full-time education or studying part time, engaged in continuous professional development or work-based learning, or perhaps studying for pleasure. You could be studying at college or university, either at a campus-based institution or at a distance, maybe overseas. Your course might be partly classroom-based, or relying on paper-based texts with an online element, or perhaps fully online. You could be a complete novice with technology or feeling pretty confident.

7

The stories here give some indication of the wide variety of students and type of situations in which they find themselves. We hope they give you a flavour of how it feels: you might see if any of them sound familiar to your own circumstances.

JENNY

Our generation has grown up with technology so we just take it all for granted.

Jenny has done well in her final school exams and has been successful in gaining a place at her university of choice. She is 18 years old and has been used to having a computer at home since she was a child. She is very confident with technology and carries her mobile phone, laptop and iPod with her wherever she goes, even on holiday. She is always connected to friends and family through email, texting, and her personal Facebook social networking site where she regularly posts messages about what she is doing and uploads digital photos to make sure everyone can share her latest exploits. She is looking forward to going to university and is keen to find out how she can enhance the skills she already has to help her to be successful when she gets there.

SALLY

All this reflection and online group discussion is interesting but I have no time for frills, I just want that degree.

Sally is a computer programmer with four dependent children. She studies in lunchtimes at work and at odd periods during the day, for example when waiting for a train to and from work, or sometimes late in the evening. Because of her job she is confident with computer use and with retrieving information from the web, but she finds essay writing hard work because it is a completely new style of writing. While she finds the course interesting and it is good to meet fellow students online, she is above all very short of time: she needs to be focused and she will just do as much as she needs to pass the course and get qualified for a new job.

PETER

Trawling through all these websites, you never know if the knowledge is actually good or not...

Seventeen-year-old Peter has recently left school and has just started at his local college. He uses his mobile phone every day for phoning, texting and accessing online news and football results. He also makes good use of its inbuilt camera to take digital photographs when he is out and about. He has access to a computer at home and uses the Internet to download music and games, as well as sending instant messages to friends who are also online. However he does not use email much as he would rather phone people than wait for them to respond to an email message. He uses Google to search for information but he knows that he cannot always trust the information he finds, and wonders if it is appropriate for his college course, and if not what the alternatives might be. In fact, he has mixed feelings about technology and is not convinced that it will help him much with his college studies. He finds on his course that he is expected to write more than he has been used to, and is having to make use of course resources, summarising and commenting on their content.

CAROLINE

Without computers and the Internet I would not have my B.Sc. (Hons) in Life Sciences. It just would not have been possible.

Caroline signed up to university study, intending to do a quick degree and improve her prospects of getting a job during the last economic downturn. Because of both cost and home commitments she chose distance learning. But only a year or so later she was hit by a debilitating illness and she is now disabled and virtually housebound. Through it all the university kept her going and gave her a goal and a hope of employment, and enabled her to fulfil her ambitions. Using a computer means that she feels less isolated: she can talk to fellow students and tutors on the forums and discuss the course she is studying. It also allows the social interaction she would otherwise lack. With the help of specialist software she can write notes and complete assignments in a fraction of the time it took previously and with a lot less discomfort. So, despite not having an employment goal, this year she decided to keep doing what she enjoys and she started a M.Sc. in Science.

YUSUF

I don't think you get anywhere if you don't know about computers. I think they're a very important part of modern living.

Yusuf is 34 years old and works full time. His employer is supporting him to attend university on a part-time basis to study for a degree. He is married with two young children and shares child care responsibilities with his partner who also works full time. He has invested in a laptop to support his studies, but is concerned about how he will fit studying around all his other commitments. He already uses computers at work to produce reports and other documents, but he is not particularly confident with the thought of writing assignments or collaborating with other students. He feels he does not have time to get heavily into computers and relies on the IT department at work to help with any technical problems which arise, which makes him a bit nervous about being responsible for his laptop at home. He recognises that time management is going to be a serious issue if he is to survive part-time study alongside all his other commitments, but he is determined to succeed because it should lead to promotion at work. He knows that he will be expected to become familiar with new digital tools and techniques for learning and would like to find out more about what these might be and how he might be expected to use them.

ANNETTE

I was very frightened of computers when I started because I thought I might crash it or I might do something terrible, you know.

Now that her children are at secondary school Annette has returned to study at college. She uses a mobile phone to keep in touch with family and friends but although there is a computer at home which her children use for playing computer games, doing homework and chatting to friends, she has never felt the need or inclination to learn how to use it. She is aware that she will have to learn to use the Internet as part of her studies as she has been told that the college has its own online learning environment, but she is feeling out of her depth among the younger students who appear to be more familiar with using technology. This is affecting her confidence about her learning but she is determined to overcome her fears, and she recognises that she has the advantage of experience in managing her time and balancing a variety of commitments. She also reads a lot and wants to make sure that she can combine her love of books with the new opportunities for information gathering that the Internet can provide.

STEPHEN

I've found my hearing loss has got a bit worse since I've got older and I find it easier to do things in a written form.

Stephen uses a computer every day at work and is highly enthusiastic about the benefits of technology. He frequently uses email at home as well as at work, uses his computer to watch TV programmes he has missed, reads topical news blogs, orders his weekly shopping and makes all his travel arrangements online. He has recently started a course of part-time study which is completely web-based. As he has a hearing impairment, he welcomes the opportunity to take part in online discussions with other students as he finds it easier to follow what is happening and to take time to reflect before contributing his views. However he realises that he will need to manage his time carefully if he is to fit study into his working and personal life. He is also concerned that he will feel isolated and alone because he will not actually be meeting his tutor and the other students on the course in a classroom.

ABOUT YOU

These student stories show that while confidence with technology is one strength, it is certainly not the end of the story. On the contrary, the extra flexibility which online use in courses can bring means that you need to be self-motivated and good at managing your time.

You too will have your own approaches to, and feelings about learning with technology, just like the students described above. If you are new to the idea, you may feel apprehensive and unsure about where to start, but it is good to recognise that we can all draw on our strengths, whether that relates to skill with technology, or to practice and experience with time management or independent study. Much will depend on the type of study you are undertaking and the extent to which your tutors design technology use into their teaching. It also depends on you, why you are studying, and what you hope to get out of it.

How We Learn 1

Some students may appreciate choice in their study and to enjoy working independently more than others do. There are many ways in which students approach their studies and that might be related to their previous experience, the reasons why they are studying, or their reaction to the college or university environment. Researchers have used the term *learning orientation* to describe the variety of student motivations, which might be *academic*, where student goals were mainly concerned with the academic side of university life, or *vocational*, where the student was concerned to get a job afterwards; *personal*, where they studied for personal satisfaction; or *social* where they were focused on socialising. Of course, this can change with circumstances, so you might have a vocational orientation at one point, and an academic orientation at another, and perhaps a combination of the two.

Source: Taylor, E., Morgan, A.R. and Gibbs, G. (1981).

Here are a few of the areas which the students in this chapter found they needed to get to grips with: you may find you also need to give these demands some thought and preparation.

Managing your learning

- You will find that time management becomes important as learning online gives you more flexibility to study at a time and place that suits you and your lifestyle.

- You will need to keep yourself motivated: this can be more challenging especially if you are not regularly meeting your classmates and tutor face-to-face.

- You will be expected to take more responsibility for managing your own learning and choosing how and when you will study.

Managing the technology

- You will need to become confident in using computers or mobile devices to write, communicate or access resources on the web.

- You may already be familiar with a web browser, email and word processing; you might also find you need to use spreadsheets, presentation software, or online forums.

- You may need to access web pages; online journal articles and e-books; graphics; photographs; and podcasts (audio) and video, or use web-based search tools to find relevant information.

- You may be asked to communicate via email, instant messaging, videoconferencing or texting; undertake group work online.

- You will certainly need to log on regularly and keep up to date with the latest course information and learning activities.

The rest of the chapters in this book give you some guidance on these areas, starting in the next chapter with the practicalities of study using online and mobile technologies.

3 Practicalities

I have only used our computer for emailing my friends and some online shopping: am slightly anxious about what I need to be able to do for my course work. Will I need a printer? I have the occasional use of one at work, but I want to do most of my study at home. How much will I need to print out? Will our Internet connection be OK for study when the kids are home and online as well?

You will certainly need to use a computer for any higher education study and if you lack confidence about using technology you may need to do a little advance planning before you start your course. There is no doubt that the use of online and mobile technologies offers students a measure of freedom and flexibility: you do not necessarily have to sit in a classroom to study, although campus-based students will be expected to attend classes as part of their course, in addition to independent study. However, this flexibility also brings with it responsibility. For example, you may need to consider where and how you will have access to a computer, the Internet or a printer. This chapter describes some of the options and gives you the opportunity to plan your time, and to consider where to start in acquiring basic IT skills.

WHAT EQUIPMENT WILL I NEED?

Computer

Whatever your course, you will need regular access to a computer with a reasonably up-to-date operating system and a reliable broadband connection. Not all students have their own equipment, and campus-based institutions commonly provide Internet access in the library, student residence or learning centre. If you are considering buying your own, you may find that your institution has negotiated special purchase deals with suppliers. You may also be eligible for an educational discount on basic software tools.

Mobile device

Many students make use of mobile devices to allow flexibility to study in different places and most use their phone to keep in touch with fellow students using SMS texting. Your mobile phone may also provide Internet access and allow you to read your email or check facts (although this can be costly) or for audio recording in lectures, or taking notes or photos during field work. It can also be very useful to set up reminders for those lectures or seminars you must attend or perhaps for assignment deadlines. Your institution might also send you text messages to remind you about dates for submitting coursework or to give you exam results. Smart phones which combine the functionality of a phone with that of a handheld computer, and laptops or netbooks provide lightweight portable computing for people who travel a lot. Finally, a personal media player such as a MP3 or MP4 player or iPod can be useful for listening to downloaded podcasts of lectures or other course material while you travel or are busy with some routine task.

Printer

There will be times when you want to print out material, particularly when you are preparing or proofreading an assignment. Printers can be expensive to maintain, and some are more suitable for drafts than for final copy. At university or college you may have to pay for printing and there will probably be a limit on the amount of printing you are entitled to do. It is worth considering how necessary it is to print a document, and whether you can manage to read and edit your written work on screen: this is certainly kinder to the environment. It is also worth having a memory stick, for temporary file backup or to transfer files for printing, as they are cheap and widely in use.

How often you need these basic tools will depend on what you are studying and where, and you will need to consult the guidance on your course. At the most basic level your tutor might expect you to have weekly access to the web to check for course resources. Other tutors might expect you to log on daily, in order to read announcements on the VLE (virtual learning environment) or take part in online forums. It will also depend on your own context and where and how study will fit into your life, as we discuss in the next section.

WHERE AND WHEN WILL I STUDY?

Studying using online media offers some flexibility in when and where you can study. Indeed, the likelihood is that you will be studying in a variety of places: here are a few options.

Study at home

There are many advantages to being able to study at home, particularly if you plan to study in evenings or weekends. You may need a space for tasks which require unbroken concentration, particularly when writing assignments. It is often an added bonus if you have family members who can help when you run into difficulties with your computer. At the same time you might need to think how you will organise your space, whether that is in a spare bedroom, or a cupboard under the stairs and in particular how you negotiate computer use or Internet access with the rest of the family, while ensuring the security and integrity of your study files.

Study in a student residence

If you live in a student residence on or near the campus you will probably have Internet access which is supported and maintained by your institution; this will give a measure of security and IT support. You may have an Internet connection point in your own room for use with your personal laptop, or a dedicated room in the residence with a limited number of shared computers, and sometimes a printer. These study spaces can also be good for undertaking study without interruptions.

Study when travelling

You may also find that you can study at odd times during the day. Like many students, you could make use of your time when travelling, perhaps while waiting for a bus or train, or sitting in a traffic jam. This can be a good opportunity for undertaking certain well-defined tasks, whether that is checking email or facts on the web, or perhaps listening to a podcast of course material, perhaps rehearsing and memorising key topics. Of course you would need to have access to the Internet-enabled laptop or mobile device which allows you to do this. You may wish to consider a mobile broadband contract which allows you to access the Internet from your laptop wherever you are, although you will need to consider the cost. Many people find that journeys can also be a great time just for thinking and planning: for which of course you need no extra equipment.

Study in the library or public access area

If you expect to make use of Internet access in a library, or in public access areas whether at the university or college or an Internet cafe, the tasks which you can do will depend on how long you are allowed to sit at a workstation, and also on your tolerance to noise and other distractions. At the same time, some people enjoy the opportunity to study in a place where they can see others working as this can be a powerful motivator, particularly when there is also free heating. In some institutions you can check online to find out how many computers are actually in use in the library, learning centre and various labs across the campus, which saves time when you are looking for a free workstation.

Study at workplace

Finally, some students study in lunch breaks in their workplace, and will use the workplace computer to do so. Short time slots provide an opportunity to keep up with email or to be in touch with fellow students on a forum. Whether you can rely on this access for undertaking longer projects like written work for an assignment will depend on your employer's policy on using their equipment and also on the amount of time you are likely to have available at work to do these learning tasks. There may also be limitations on the websites which you are able to visit from an intranet, or indeed to any specialist software which you might need for your course. Organisational firewalls which are designed to protect the workplace against malicious attack may restrict audio or video conferencing over the Internet when working from the office.

GOOD PRACTICE WHEREVER YOU STUDY

Always keep backup copies of important files. You could use a memory stick or save files to the server of your university, college or Internet service provider if you are allowed to do so, or on free web-based file-sharing sites.

Store your favourite web links in social bookmarking sites. This means you can access them from any computer and even choose to share them with fellow students.

Using your own computer

Viruses arrive in emails and downloads. Ensure your virus protection is up to date, so that you do not suffer from, or pass on malicious software.

However, anti-virus is not as important now as anti-malware and firewalls. Spyware and other malware can come from visiting a dodgy website, or a free web service which is supported by advertising, so make sure you have adequate protection: there is software which you can download from the web. You may find that your institution recommends specific software for this, or you can use *Spybot* and *AdAware* (both freeware, though you can pay for extra functions) http://www.safer-networking.org; http://www.lavasoft.com/.

Be aware that free public file-sharing sites should be used with caution and can be a conduit for viruses, adware and spyware. They can also make files on your computer available to other people, turning your computer into a server unless you specifically tell them not to. You should always check privacy regulations and make sure your personal details are only seen by those you choose to share them with. Read some good advice from the UK government *Getsafeonline* site on file-sharing sites (http://www.getsafeonline.org).

Identify in advance where you can find technical support should the need arise. This might come from your Internet service provider, an online support centre, other technically-savvy friends or relatives, or a local computer repair service. Some university or college IT services can provide assistance, for example the institution may wish you to use a specific virus protection package or a suite of office software tools which they can provide at reduced cost or even free of charge.

Study in public space

Always remember to log out fully from a shared computer when you have completed your session, especially if you have logged in using your own ID and password. This will ensure that the next user cannot access any of your personal details or view restricted websites. If you are at a cafe or other uncontrolled station check for USB keyloggers and other devices which secretly note your key strokes, and if you are unhappy with the environment, do not use it for anything sensitive.

When at home negotiate how you will share space and equipment with other members of the family. Consider setting up a wireless network in your home so that different members of the family can be online at the same time as you are yourself from anywhere in the house. If you share a computer, keep your study files in a distinctive place on the computer's hard drive which other family members do not use.

Study at workplace

If your employer is supporting your study, it may be useful to talk through access to websites, the use of specialist software, or institutional firewalls with the IT department well in advance of starting the course to find out if they will be willing to help you overcome any unexpected technical problems. Having an agreement on how much time you can use for study at work is also helpful.

Plan your time

Now it is time to do a little planning. You might need to consider how much time you have each week for study and where you will be during that time. You certainly need to know how you will access the Internet and where you expect to do your assignments. You may wish to plan where you can use a printer.

> ### *Try This*
> We have produced a table with some imaginary entries: you may find helpful to complete it with your own comments.
>
> | Where | When | For what | Comments |
> |---|---|---|---|
> | Work | Lunchtimes Mon–Fri | Internet access to email and websites | Great high-speed network and technician on tap, but I only have ½ hour per day |
> | Home | Evenings Tues and Thurs | Report and essay writing; reflective contributions to forums, e-portfolios, blogs or wikis | Tues and Thurs are quiet times for writing, because kids are out, but Internet sometimes dodgy |
> | Internet cafe | When I am travelling | Internet access | Hopeless for thinking if it is noisy; expensive if you stay too long |

DISTRACTIONS AND EFFECTIVE ONLINE STUDY

One of the challenges of online study is that it can be full of distractions. You may already be aware that it is easy to go online to read about one topic, and then to find yourself an hour later still browsing the web, having forgotten your original goal. Perhaps you have had the experience of answering one email and then being unable to resist reading and responding to several others. You might send a short message in a chat

forum on a social networking site, and then find yourself engaged
in totally unrelated communication with others who happen to be
connected at the same time. You may have downloaded a podcast of a
radio programme that relates to your studies, but the temptation to listen
to some music on your MP3 player instead proves too strong. Some people
are very adept at 'multi-tasking' and can deal effectively with several
activities at once, as Pete comments:

> *I was doing my blog and doing my homework for economics all at the same
> time and listening to music in the background, thinking 'who says men
> can't multitask?!'*

Others may find they need to focus on one activity at a time if they are to
complete a learning task effectively. You will need to manage your time
in a way that is going to allow you to concentrate on meaningful writing,
reading or listening without too many distractions. This means that you
should think carefully about how you fit your study into your routine.

Try This

How do you cope with multi-tasking? Which of these statements applies to
you?

- I like to read in silence with no distractions.
- I prefer to have music playing while I read.
- Noise doesn't disturb me as I can easily shut out other distractions.
- I like to read or listen while I'm on the bus, train or in the car.
- I like to listen while I'm walking, running or in the gym.
- I prefer to turn off Instant Messaging and social networking if I'm doing coursework.
- I quite like stopping regularly for a break to check the web, reading a few blogs when I'm reading serious stuff online or writing an assignment.
- If I'm going to concentrate on a podcast I need a quiet place where I can take notes.

Thinking about the answers to these questions will help you to decide which
techniques might be best for you. But see this as a starting point and be
prepared to change your mind as you become more confident in studying
online. You may well find that your answers will change with the level and
type of course you study, and also the importance, and urgency, of the study
tasks you engage in. Be open-minded about approaches you may not have
considered before.

WHAT IT SKILLS WILL I NEED?

If you are fairly new to using a computer, you will certainly find it helpful
to be familiar with some basic skills which we list below. You might like
to tick the skills you already have, and make plans to find out about those
which you need to develop.

Basic IT skills	Can do	Need to practise
Keyboard skills		
Using a mouse		
Moving and resizing windows		
Creating and saving documents • formatting text • spellchecking • copying, cutting and pasting • inserting tables and graphics • cropping and resizing graphics • naming files electronic filing		
Printing		
Using a web browser		
Using a search engine		
Emailing and attaching files		
Downloading and saving files		

A wide range of online courses are available to develop these skills, alternatively a course at your local college will give you the opportunity to learn with help readily to hand.

Sites for Practising Basic IT Skills

BBC Computer Tutor – introducing use of mouse, keyboard and computer screen:

http://www.bbc.co.uk/computertutor

Webguide: an Open University guide to effective use of the web:

http://www.open.ac.uk/webguide/

Online *Touchtyping* practice:

http://www.sense-lang.org/typing/

Learn Direct: a wide range of online courses on using a computer:

http://www.learndirect.co.uk/

Self-study materials on using a computer for study:

http://www.caledonian.ac.uk/student/ictskills/material/

http://www.open.ac.uk/pc4study

Tutorials for using *OpenOffice* and *Microsoft Office:*

http://www.tutorialsforopenoffice.org

http://www.homeandlearn.co.uk

(All web links are listed at the back of the book, and on our book website at: http://sites.google.com/site/learnonlinegroup/).

If you are expected to use specific tools as part of your study, for example online databases of books and journals, a VLE such as Moodle or Blackboard, online referencing tools, complex spreadsheets, graphics or computer-aided design software, then it is usual for training to be provided by your institution. You will also find fellow students on your course who are already familiar with new techniques and who are willing to share their experiences. You too can become a valuable source of expertise for others as you become more confident yourself.

21

FINAL COMMENTS

We hope you can see that study using online and mobile technologies will offer plenty of advantages in terms of flexibility, but that you need to plan to accommodate the practicalities of studying in a variety of places, with a range of tools. The rest of the book describes the various processes of study which you will encounter in higher education, and illustrates the ways in which they can be supported using online and mobile technologies.

4 Listening, Reading and Sense-making

I used to wonder how I could possibly have got to the end of that first module without a clue as to what it had been about. But I am learning, at least, I'm learning how to survive. Once I discovered how much it helped to go over the main points more than once by downloading and reading over the handouts and listening to the podcast, I started to get the gist of what it was about then at least I had a fighting chance.

We are surrounded by sounds, whether from people's voices, mobile phones, traffic noise, television, radio or MP3 players. We also read books, newspapers, magazines, email, text messages, web pages, adverts, even cereal packets, but the extent to which we retain a memory of what we read or hear, or gain a sense that the knowledge has changed our thinking in some way really depends on the context and the reasons why we are reading or listening to it in the first place. While this is probably not important for cereal packets, it is certainly an issue for effective study at college or university.

Technology has made it possible to present course content in a range of innovative ways. This chapter will explain what you might encounter and how it might help you in effective listening, reading and sense-making.

COURSE CONTENT AND THE IMPACT OF TECHNOLOGIES

All courses, whether they are studied at university or college contain course content, that is, knowledge about the subject which students are expected to understand and occasionally to learn by heart: and depending on the course, that content might be knowledge about everyday life in mediaeval times, or plant biology, or perhaps musical notation. In addition to subject knowledge are various skills which you will need to practise, for example in problem solving and communication skills, or maybe the proper way to give an injection, or to use the right statistical test for experimental data, or the appropriate tense in a foreign language. The whole process of learning in a certain way in a particular discipline also takes some time to become familiar with, whether you are reading mathematical notation or a social sciences text. Whatever form it takes, this core course content is of central interest to all students for the simple reason that it is likely to be the material on which coursework and final assessment is based.

For students who attend campus, course content has traditionally been presented in lectures, where lecturers may explain concepts or inject enthusiasm for the subject, supported by course texts. For distance students this content is delivered in course texts and books, whether online or in printed form, or through additional digital resources.

For campus-based courses, technologies have a potentially dramatic impact both on what lecturers can do in delivering content and what students can do in reading, listening to and making sense of that content. At the simplest level, online handouts or presentations made available before or after the lecture can give campus-based students extra flexibility in when they study.

Perhaps more excitingly, some lecturers have moved to a completely new type of course design. Such courses encourage you to take a more active approach to learning by including online activities and discussion with fellow students, or perhaps interactive animations and simulations. But the story does not end there, because there is so much educational material freely available on the web that you can easily add to the core material your course provides. You may also be asked to contribute to the course resources using data or other material you may have gathered or created yourself or with others. These developments are common both to study at a campus-based university and study at a distance, and effectively mean that the student experience of campus-based study need no longer be so radically different from distance education, although as a distance student you might miss out on that drink at the bar with friends.

THE USE OF ONLINE OR MOBILE TOOLS FOR COURSE CONTENT

Tools you might use:

File-sharing sites; podcasts; electronic voting; quizzes and simulations; virtual worlds

In this section we deal with lecture materials first, then move on to courses where the content is wholly or partly online.

Online lecture materials

Lecturers often provide online access to notes or slide presentations either before or after a lecture, tutorial or lab session. In some cases this covers the lecture material, but it may also contain extra reading or preparation material before the lecture. These handouts are made available from the VLE, or from public file-sharing sites: either way they can be accessed from any Internet-connected device.

Slideshare is a publicly available file-sharing site which specialises in providing space for presentations. You can choose whether to share your presentation with a private group, or whether to make it publicly available. http://www. slideshare.net

(All web links are listed at the back of the book, and on our book website at: http://sites.google.com/site/learnonlinegroup/).

As an alternative, some lecturers record their lectures or provide shorter 'soundbite' pieces on key topics and make them available as downloadable *podcasts*. Podcasts are audio recordings, sometimes in a series which can be subscribed to so that they are downloaded automatically whenever there is a new recording in the series. Podcasts can be either played direct from the website or downloaded on to a computer to play later, or transferred to a mobile device. They allow you to listen again to course material in your own time, and are particularly helpful if you are dyslexic or have impaired vision, since you can study at your own pace without relying on the printed word.

Some podcasts also include video or integrate both audio and video within a presentation: often called *vidcasts, webcasts* or *vodcasts*. They are particularly useful where the lecturer needs to refer to diagrams or illustrations while they are talking.

You will find many good examples of educational podcasts, as well as on-off audio recordings on *iTunesU*, dubbed as 'the campus that never sleeps', which contains a growing collection from various universities around the world. You will need to download the iTunes software from the website before you can explore what is available. Some podcasts can only be downloaded by students from the university where the podcast came from, others are available to all. http://www.iTunesU.com

Before we leave lectures and campus-based study you may encounter some lecturers who make use of *electronic voting systems*. Each student is given a handset which is rather like a remote control device. They are asked to vote by pressing the appropriate button, in response to a question posed by the lecturer. The responses of the whole class are collated automatically and displayed on a screen, giving everybody a good measure of the class's understanding of key topics. This process is a useful way to identify which topics you may have to spend some more time on.

Online courses

When course content is written specifically for online delivery it looks completely different to what you would see in a traditional lecture handout or printed textbook. The text is often arranged in shorter sections which are hot linked, so the experience of reading on screen becomes less linear than it would be when reading a document or book. You can locate and focus on those parts of the text which are particularly important, or click on links to further reading when you wish to follow up an area of interest in more detail.

Open2.net the learning portal of the BBC and the Open University (UK) contains a range of easy web-based tutorials on various topical subjects which provide a good example of online content design in small chunks, with thought provoking activities you can try out.

http://www.open2.net/learning/ then click on the 'Learning' tab.

Content which is delivered wholly or mostly online is generally designed to be read on the screen, whether that is on a computer, or mobile device. Reading from a screen differs from reading from paper in several important ways. We know for example that reading speed is reduced, so it takes longer to read the same content on screen than it does on paper. At the same time the font size can be altered to suit your eyesight, and you can search for specific words, or perhaps use a screen reader to get the text to read out loud. Reading on a mobile device is different again because the screen is smaller, and new standards are emerging for text which is designed specifically for dedicated e-book readers, or alternatively for reading on other mobile devices, like smart phones.

On some courses you may undertake activities and find things out for yourself instead of reading all the content from one source. That might involve searching and researching the web, or getting involved in online collaborative activities and discussion with fellow students. Learning tasks or activities may also take place away from the computer, using mobile devices for fieldwork or work-based learning. For example in geological sciences mobile devices are used for recording data and communicating it, or making notes, as well as using a global positioning system (GPS) for locating geological sites. On other courses you may be required to undertake interviews, and use your mobile device for recording or for taking photographs.

For particularly difficult parts of the course you may encounter *quizzes* or *simulations*. Quizzes can be an ideal way of illustrating or modelling difficult concepts, providing the opportunity to practise and repeat activities over and over until you have a grasp of the concept. The quiz often provides helpful feedback on your efforts.

Try This

The Open University (UK) is making use of formative quizzes in many of its courses. You can see how they work by visiting 'Are you ready for Science?' and select 'Interactive Materials'. See how ready you are for study at: http://www.open.ac.uk/science/courses-qualifications/are-you-ready-for-science/ then select 'Interactive Materials'.

Simulations can provide students with the opportunity to try out 'what if' questions to see the result, and can be particularly useful if you are learning about hazardous procedures or a topic which is otherwise difficult to visualise.

Visible Body© is a visualisation tool which displays human anatomy in fully interactive 3D. http://www.visiblebody.com

---

Other more ambitious options are already beginning to make an impact on education. These include *3D virtual worlds*, which are games-like environments where you create a character or avatar to represent yourself 'in-world' as you interact with your new surroundings and the other avatars you meet on the way. Many universities and colleges are building novel learning environments in these virtual worlds. Activities include role-play, online tutorials for distance students, creative activities for art and design students, or simulations for engineering and health-related subjects. The example in Figure 4.1 shows a virtual clinical skills lab in Second Life where student nurses learn about decision making processes as they work with virtual patients who can react as unpredictably as real ones.

FINAL COMMENTS

We hope this has given you an overview of the many possibilities you may encounter when listening to or reading course content. We should point out that students often make use of resources beyond core course content, and the extent to which this material can be used for study is discussed in Chapter 8 on 'Searching and researching'.

Figure 4.1   A virtual clinical skills lab in Second Life

Source: Reproduced with kind permission from the CUThere team at Glasgow Caledonian University (http://www.gcal.ac.uk/cuthere/).

In the next chapter we go on to discuss good practice in using technologies for listening, reading and sense-making.

5 Listening, Reading and Sense-making: A Survival Guide

I used to make conscientious notes, but as I moved jobs I made less and less notes because of time pressures. During the course as I'm studying I think 'here is something I want to learn and need to understand'. If there is any tuning it's for assignments, I mark sections as I go along and write notes in my word processor which might be of relevance to the next assignment. It's all a question of focus and deciding on the purpose, the reason why you are listening to or reading this stuff and what you want to get out of it.

29

Many online and mobile tools can help you to listen, read and make sense of course material, while offering some extra flexibility in study routines. They can also connect you to others with whom you can share ideas and test your understanding.

This chapter focuses on effective approaches to the study of core course content with the help of online and mobile technologies. We start the chapter with 'making sense' of course material, because after all that is the central purpose of studying.

MAKING SENSE OF COURSE MATERIAL

You might imagine that reading course texts or listening to a lecture will be fairly passive activities in which you focus your attention on soaking up new information presented by the writer or lecturer. However this is not going to be a particularly effective strategy and is unlikely to help you to develop a real understanding of the subject.

How We Learn 2

When researchers asked students: 'What do you mean by learning?' the students came up with a variety of responses or *conceptions*. Some felt it meant increasing knowledge, or memorising, or acquiring facts. In contrast other students described it as abstracting meaning, understanding reality or developing as a person. In a related study researchers described a variety of ways in which students read as *deep, surface or strategic* approaches. A deep approach to learning is when students develop an understanding of underlying principles and an ability to apply knowledge to new situations. A surface approach is what happens with rote learning and memorising, where students quickly forget the facts they have learnt, and have a limited understanding of the subject. A strategic approach means that they are learning enough in order to pass the next assignment or exam, or maybe just playing the system. Students might adopt different approaches at different times according to the circumstances, so they could adopt a deep approach when studying a subject for which they have a particular personal interest, and maybe a strategic approach before an exam for a boring but necessary qualification.

Source: Saljo, R. (1979); Marton, F. and Saljo, R. (1997).

There are no doubt times when you need to memorise facts which are often basic building blocks for your subject, for example vocabulary in a foreign language or mathematical formulae. At other times you will be under pressure to pass an exam. However, if you wish to aim for deep learning and a more rounded understanding of your subject, then you need to consider ways of doing something active with the course content, and that is what we mean here by sense-making. You will need to develop your understanding of the subject by linking it to knowledge you already have and relating it to your own experiences.

Aims and expectations

There are several ways in which you can be effective at sense-making, whether you are reading course texts or listening to a lecturer. We will start with your aims and expectations. It is a good idea to have a clear idea of your purpose in listening or reading, what you expect to get out of it, and some idea of the author or lecturer's intention. Try to focus on important ideas and theories, so that you aim for an overview of the subject, which you will need to revise as your understanding develops. The detail can be 'attached' to the mental framework you construct. The educational researchers who described deep and surface approaches to learning made a useful comment on students' different ways of reading course texts:

> *What we found was that the students who did not get 'the point' failed to do so simply because they were not looking for it ... what the text was about: the author's intention, the main point, the conclusion to be drawn.*

Marton, F. and Saljo, R. (1997, p. 43)

You are likely at some point to come across parts of the course which you find really difficult to understand, either because the ideas are completely unlike anything you have met before, or you cannot relate them to any of your previous experience, or they are just plain complicated, and you might wonder what to do about it. Sometimes you may feel you have reached a point when you think 'Aha' and can see what the subject was all about. The fact is that you might need to return to some topics several times before you start to understand them fully, and this can be quite worrying. The important thing is to be aware that this happens to most students, and to be ready to identify what it is you find difficult. You may find it helps to backtrack and revisit the material, or seek clarification by doing some additional reading, or ask your tutor or lecturer for some explanation.

How We Learn 3

You may come across 'Big Moments' in learning about a course which can lead you to view the subject in a completely new way. They are known as *Threshold concepts*. You might even find that you feel different yourself when you reach that 'penny dropping moment' and have reached a rounded understanding. It can take some time to get there, and students often find that they need to make a number of attempts to get to grips with these concepts, with a few blind alleys along the way. Altogether it can be pretty nerve wracking. You may encounter aspects of the course which trip you up because they might not relate to anything you have been familiar with in the past, or maybe they are just really difficult to understand – that is known as *Troublesome Knowledge*.

Source: Meyer, J.H.F. and Land, R. (2006); Perkins, D. (1999).

Many students find that the time when they finally start to reach a deeper understanding of what the course is about is during the revision period before the exam. Simply by concentrating on re-reading course material, working through a variety of sources and discussing issues with fellow students, you can begin to see the connections between different parts of the course and see the subject as a whole in new ways. So although exams can be a pretty stressful experience the preparation for them can have important benefits. Jonathan explains what he likes to do during revision:

When I'm revising I will be using my word processor to summarise the notes I made already. Sometimes I record myself too: I read the summary out loud and make a recording on my mobile, I often remember things when I've done that and played it back to myself.

GOOD PRACTICE GUIDELINES

Note taking

Tools you might use

Word processor; mind maps

A good sense-making approach is to develop your understanding by writing about it. Taking notes is probably the most common method: that involves jotting down key points which act as a reference point from which you can seek further information or share your ideas with others. There is no point in trying to write down everything you read or hear because you will fail. Sometimes the notes can be useful for writing coursework, as you draw together what you have learnt over the module and semester and begin to see how the various strands relate to each other.

If you have a laptop or mobile device, you could type up these key points while you are reading or listening. You can always return to them later, making use of the highlighter or special fonts to bring out important points. Some students like to add illustrations or graphs which they have cut and pasted from electronic resources: if properly attributed (that means including details of where you found them) they can be used as examples.

You may find it helpful to construct a glossary of any new terms you come across. You could also build up a list of web links and references from course reading lists which you can annotate with notes on their usefulness: this can be handy for future assignments.

Mind mapping is an alternative to writing notes, and can be particularly helpful when you are revising for exams and trying to draw together the different parts of the course. Once in digital form the mind map can be edited with further information, linked to further sources and resources on the web, or shared with friends. Software for mind mapping can be downloaded from the web: while most are priced, many packages offer a free trial period.

Specialist tools such as *MindManager* or open source option *Freemind* and many others can help to create nodes and make connections between them in ways that may help stimulate creativity and imagination. http://www.mindjet.com; http://sourceforge.net

(All web links are listed at the back of the book, and on our book website at: http://sites.google.com/site/learnonlinegroup/).

File storage

Tools you might use

Memory stick; file-sharing service; mobile device; social bookmarking; e-portfolios

It is essential to back up files if they contain information which you cannot afford to lose. This means that if your own computer breaks down, you have not lost all the material and writing which you collected for your next assignment. You might use a mobile device for notes or copy your notes files to a memory stick, carry them around with you and read them from any computer. Alternatively you can store files online which makes it easy to develop and share your writing with fellow students, whether that is a course glossary, or mind map, or list of web links: they are then in a place where everyone can access them. A common option is the *e-portfolio* which is available in some universities and colleges and provides a personal web space on the institution's server where you can keep your files, and share them with others if you wish.

An alternative, and in the public domain, are file-sharing services which allow anyone to save and share files, but be aware that there are security issues in using public filesharing which we discuss in Chapter 3.

Google Docs is a free web-based word processor and spreadsheet and file-sharing site which can be used to share the development of documents, regardless of your location. http://www.docs.google.com

Many file-sharing services are specialised for particular types of resource, for example *Flickr* which is used for images and *YouTube* for video http://www.flickr.com; http://www.youtube.com.

Finally, if you are collecting and sharing lists of resources you might wish to use a social bookmarking site, and we refer you to Chapter 8 for further details.

Learning diary

Tools you might use

Blogs; e-portfolios; mobile device

Some students find that writing thoughts in a learning diary can help them to make sense of new ideas and experiences. In fact on some courses this is an official requirement, and may even be assessed. Blogs provide an easy way of publishing news and reflection as Falicity has done here.

Time and Tide

Monday, February 23

Getting behind

I had great plans for getting something done tonight but I ended up working a 17hr shift yesterday, got 5 hours sleep then back to work this morning so I'm now lying on my couch with my duvet!! No study tonight I'm afraid!! I chose a distance course as I work obscure hours and can't regularly attend a class. Time off is a big problem for me. Must try harder tomorrow…need to get that assignment finished by Saturday.

POSTED BY FELICITY BROUGHAM 9 comments
<< Home

Figure 5.1   Use of a blog for a learning diary

Joan finds her reflective diary is becoming more useful as she gets used to writing it:

> *I write a learning diary and I do try to reflect, but it is really hard sometimes to write about your feelings, how you feel, not just about what you learnt or what you did. I think it does help my learning and it does get easier the more you do, just with practice I think I've got better at it.*

You might wish to experiment with an audio diary. Trying to explain things is one of the best ways to discover how well you understand them yourself. This can be particularly appropriate if you are undertaking work-based learning, and need to record thoughts and ideas as you move about the workplace. It can make a refreshing change from jotting down notes, although you might think twice before attempting this during a lecture. You could make use of your mobile phone or other mobile device to record the entries, or use recording software on your computer.

Audacity is a freely available tool for recording and editing sounds which can be downloaded to your computer. You will need a microphone in order to record yourself. http://audacity.sourceforge.net.

Your learning diary can form part of personal development planning using your *e- portfolio* which allows you to keep a reflective account of your learning and gather evidence of your success. This might consist of assessment results and tutor feedback, an inventory of skills and experiences gained through placements as part of your course or part-time employment, any work experiences and CV, all of which is valuable when seeking employment at a later stage. Many universities and colleges provide such tools either as part of their VLE or through specialist software packages.

Quick tips: note-taking and reflection (word processor; e-portfolio; file-sharing sites; mind maps; blogs; mobile device)

- Seek out the main points in course content;
- Type up or speak the main points in your own words;
- Experiment with a mind map as a change from notes;
- Include your own comments if you are writing reflections;
- Add links and illustrations from web resources;
- Create a glossary of terms used in the course;
- Save your notes and reflections on a memory stick or in your e-portfolio so they are accessible wherever you study;
- Consider sharing and developing your notes, mind map, glossary or web links with fellow students: that can help to build your understanding.

35

Reading

Tools you might use

Web browser; word processor; mobile device

The comments we have already made on sense-making in this chapter apply here and it is good to get an idea of the overall gist of what you are reading before you worry about the detail. To do this, check the contents list or perhaps look at the headings in the paper, website or chapter. In this way you will gain a sense of the author's intentions, and give yourself a mental picture of the subject area. You might also make some decisions on which areas are most important to read, and what might be left until another time. As you read it is worth asking yourself a few questions about the text, and it is good to compare and evaluate what you read with other parts of the course, or alternatively with other resources you may have read previously. And if you get stuck with a section of text, try revisiting earlier sections which may build on the sticky area, or read on to the next section which may set it all in context.

When reading on screen the tool you use and the file format will define how you can study. You will find a list of file formats with their abbreviations in Appendix B. Read-only Acrobat (.pdf) files which cannot be altered are often used to send articles and course information to students. At other times you will read from web pages and standard read/write (.doc) files.

If you want to be selective about the parts of text which you read, you can use the links embedded in web pages to move around to different sections, or alternatively use the contents page in a .pdf file just as you would in a printed book. You can also search for significant words and phrases within a document or web page. As you read, you may wish to highlight sections of text in a document which are worth returning to later. If the course text is a read/write document (.doc) file, you can open the 'Reviewing' pane and type your comments directly into the document.

Try This

To get a flavour of reading a book on screen, visit *Planet*, the pdf user community, and download a free book from the website. You will need a recent version of *Adobe Acrobat* on your computer, which can also be downloaded from the site. You could try searching for specific words, changing the font size, or getting the book to read itself to you. http://www.planetpdf.com.

Reading from the screen or printing it out is very much a matter of personal preference, as Ebony comments:

> *I don't like sitting in front of the computer for ages and having to read it all so I print it off and then read it again. I don't feel that I can take it all in just by sitting in front of the computer reading it all.*

Other students like reading from the screen and if you have your own laptop you can download documents and read them on screen wherever you happen to be. Some universities provide course texts in a format suitable for e-book readers, and this can be another flexible way to read course material at a convenient time, provided you possess an e-book reader.

The type of information you are reading may also influence your decision. Many people prefer to print out longer documents whereas they will be happy to read web-based information which has been specially written in smaller 'chunks' for online consumption. Heidi certainly prefers this:

> *For things like the news I'm quite happy to read it on the Internet. I read more news on the Internet than I do from the papers.*

Presentations can often have animations or added layers of diagrams or graphs which will not display in the same way when they are printed out. They may also have integrated notes, video or audio which have to be watched or listened to on a computer.

Finally, there may be parts of the course which you need to repeat or learn more thoroughly especially during revision. Very often it helps if you can carry this information around with you, and rehearse or practise while waiting for a bus or doing the ironing, so you might consider downloading either text or a sound file to a mobile device.

Quick tips: reading (word processor; web browser; presentation software; mobile device)

- Get the gist first: look at contents and main headings;
- When you are stuck, backtrack to an earlier section or read further;
- To read selectively on screen:
    - search for significant words
    - look at contents list
    - use hyperlinks;
- When note taking from material on screen:
    - open separate word processing page
    - highlight relevant sections of text
    - use reviewing pane to comment on text in a word document;
- When rehearsing important facts:
    - download content to mobile device and play it back to yourself;
- Print sparingly;
- For revision and memorising key points consider transferring small chunks of material to a mobile device and carry it around with you.

Listening

Tools you might use

Word processor; mobile device; podcasts or vidcasts

Students who attend campus may be expected to spend a considerable time in listening, whether that is to lectures, guest speakers,

presentations from fellow students, questions and answers, debates
and discussions, and it can often be difficult to concentrate for lengthy
periods. Our comments on strategies for effective sense-making apply
here and you will probably find that you really need to take notes while
you are listening.

Your lecturers may be willing to allow digital recordings to be made
of their lectures, but ask permission first. Others themselves provide
podcasts or vidcasts. To benefit from audio recordings you will need
access to a computer with a sound card and speakers or personal
headphones.

> Freely available software tools such as *Windows Media* or *Quicktime* can cope
> with both sounds and moving images. http://www.microsoft.com/windows/
> windowsmedia/default.mspx; http://www.apple.com/uk/quicktime/

Podcasts can be downloaded to a mobile device for listening at odd times
of the day. Bruce likes listening while he walks:

> *I always have my phone and iPod with me. With an iPod you can listen
> to study material when you're on the go. If you're walking somewhere you
> can do it.*

Other students like to make notes or perhaps refer to course materials
while listening to podcasts, so you might need to find a space and time
to do that.

Where lecture materials are available before lectures or tutorials, you
can prepare in advance. This means that instead of spending time
taking detailed notes in the lecture or tutorial, you will be in a position
to listen more closely, paying special attention to the aspects which
you are less sure about and asking questions about them. As Jonathan
commented:

> *If you only get time to listen to something once you maybe think 'I didn't
> get any of those answers at all', but you can go home and you can listen to
> it as many times as you like so its very useful.*

There are always advantages in making the most of 'live' lectures and
tutorials for asking questions, and for pacing yourself and keeping up
with deadlines, and of course for meeting fellow students and feeling
that you are part of the class.

> **Quick tips: listening (word processor; memory stick; podcasts)**
>
> - Listen for key points, and make a note of them;
> - save your notes to a memory stick, add to them later;
> - make use of lecturer's podcasts to get the gist before you attend the lecture or tutorial;
> - take notes as you listen to podcasts, and note questions you need to ask;
> - make use of the lecture/tutorial to ask those questions and check your understanding.

ADAPTATIONS TO YOUR COMPUTER

One of the great advantages of writing and reading using a computer is that you can adjust the display to suit your requirements. Simple adaptations can help to reduce strain if you find keyboard activity or screen reading difficult, particularly if you have dyslexia or a visual impairment.

> **Quick tips: adaptations for reading and writing**
>
> - Adjust the font size. When reading text from a screen adjust the size of the font so that it becomes comfortably legible. You can make an adjustment within your word processor, or within a web page.
> - Try comparing pages. Many word processors have a setting which allows you to read pages side by side, like a book. This can be very helpful if you have a long paper to read, and wish to compare one part of text with another.
> - Voice-activated software allows you to speak what you wish to write, and the program converts your thoughts into written text. Some students find that this can be a very good way of getting their text to flow. However it takes time to train your system to recognise your voice and therefore you need to allow some time before your course starts to develop an appropriate level of expertise.
> - Screen readers speak the text from the screen, and can be useful for students with visual impairment. Some websites and pdf readers have this facility as a standard.

FINAL COMMENTS

You will need to experiment with the tools available to you to ensure that you are reading and listening in a way that makes best use of your time while developing your understanding. We cannot emphasise enough the importance of adopting active approaches to study, and the following chapters go on to discuss the many ways in which you can do this, whether you are communicating with fellow students, searching for further resources or writing assignments.

While we have discussed some aspects of making sense of course content in this chapter, we know that you will also find many useful ideas in other parts of this book. So, for example, online discussion with fellow students is often important for making sense of course material, and we refer you to Chapter 6 on 'Communicating and community'. Preparing and writing assignments or the exam are also important ways in which students make sense of course material, and this topic is dealt with in Chapter 10 on 'Writing and presenting'.

6 Communicating and Community

I plucked up the courage to see what the others were saying on the forum. There's time to think what you want to say, things I would never have said on the phone. You're trying other things all the time, it's another way of communicating. This is a superb way of working remotely. I wish our company did this. Having written comments rather than speaking them in a meeting you can't interpret the meeting differently... Success depends on people regularly logging on. If you are working to a deadline, things need to be moved along.

41

Everyday life is full of opportunities to communicate, and increasingly much of this takes place online. While some of us make use of email to keep in touch with friends, and often dread the numbers of emails we receive for work, others are used to keeping in touch throughout the day with their friends, using instant messaging or social networking.

Some people like blogging and publishing news about their particular interests, or perhaps reading and commenting on others' blogs. Communicating online is no longer restricted to home or office, because mobile devices allow us to combine phone use with the ability to check email or websites in addition to talking or texting.

This chapter shows you why and how communicating and belonging to a community with your fellow students is important for study at university or college, and describes the various tools which are available to support this, together with some examples of the many ways in which they are used.

COMMUNICATING FOR STUDY

The use of online and mobile technologies has had a major impact on how we communicate and also on who we contact and when. Not only is it common to keep in touch with friends and colleagues on a far more continuous basis than ever before, it has also become possible to contact people who would otherwise be unavailable, whether because of their geography, or their status at work, or because we had never met them before: people have simply become more accessible.

Communicating with a student group is one of the most important parts of studying. You might think this is rather an odd thing to say: surely study is about reading, or listening to a lecture or tutorial? But we know that if you want to learn effectively, then you not only need to hear or read about new concepts, you need to do something active with them. That might involve relating new information to your previous experience, and what you have already learnt. It can also mean that you share these ideas and discuss them with others.

There is another major reason for communicating: it is a great way of joining and belonging to a community. Whether you attend a campus or work at a distance, studying can be isolating, and many students find that they can begin to lose motivation if they do not have the opportunity to meet each other and find out how others are doing. Joining an online group can make student life that bit more fun: it can be enough just to keep you going. It gives you connections with fellow students which can supplement the support which is provided by your tutor, and means that you need not feel isolated even if you are unable to meet up with other students regularly. It means that there is help when you get stuck, and you may find others who are having difficulties which are similar to your own. If you study at unsocial hours, and particularly if you are a part-time student, you can still keep in touch with fellow students and with tutors. You are no longer completely on your own.

How We Learn 4

We all have a different understanding of what we read which is coloured by the experiences and beliefs we have had in the past. There is little doubt that sharing ideas and testing them out with others can be a very powerful way of deepening understanding. *Social constructivist* theories maintain that the development of understanding takes place when individuals attempt to make sense of new information by relating it to familiar experiences, and by using conversational language to discuss ideas and understanding of course concepts with fellow students.

Source: Jonassen, D. H. et al. (1995); Pask, G. (1975).

TOOLS FOR COMMUNICATING

Tools you might use

Email; SMS; social networking; instant messaging; VOIP; forums; blogs; micro-blogs; web conferencing

You may already be using various technologies in everyday life which can be useful to support your study. Of those particularly concerned with communication, email, instant messaging and social networking sites are probably the most common. Although you may already have your own email account, most institutions provide a special email account to use for study. For social networking you will very often find that sites like Facebook have groups which are set up for students from your college or university. Instant messaging or online chat is commonly used for keeping in touch with fellow students and is standard provision on most computers. Software which allows you to make voice calls through your computer using voice over internet protocol (VOIP) is also widely available and easy to download from the web. This can be very useful for contact between students and for keeping in touch with family and friends at a distance at little or no cost, although some institutions do not encourage its use on campus because it can slow down access for other users.

> *Skype* uses VOIP protocol and is easy to download from the web. http://www.skype.com/intl/en-gb/
>
> (All web links are listed at the back of the book, and on our book website at: http://sites.google.com/site/learnonlinegroup/).

Most colleges and universities also provide a virtual learning environment (VLE) which integrates tools of particular value for learning. Your access to some or all of these applications will depend on the VLE and how your course and institution make use of it, but we describe here some of the more commonly used communication tools.

The most widely used tool for group communication at college or university is the discussion forum. A forum works rather like email, except that instead of mailing one or two people, your message goes to a group, and anyone in the group may reply.

In contrast to this group discussion is the monologue which you encounter in a blog (short for web log). Blogs provide a simple way of publishing news and events and often commentary, or sometimes an online diary. You may already be aware of the many journalists, politicians, academics and socially active individuals who use these effectively to share their views with the public.

> ### *Try This*
>
> To get a flavour of the uses for blogs, have a look at the comments page in your newspaper or TV and radio news websites. Many journalists maintain their own blog, in addition to writing articles, and it is generally mentioned at the end of their column or web page.

Blogs do not just contain text entries, they can also include photos, video or podcasts. The most recent entries in the blog are usually at the top of the screen, and there is generally a place at the end of each entry for readers to comment, if they wish. Each entry may have tags, a list of keywords which identify the content, and most blogs have links to other blogs dealing with similar content.

> Your university or college may provide access to blogs for students, but if not, there are many freely available tools such as *Blogger* or *WordPress*.
>
> http://www.blogger.com; http://wordpress.org

A variation on the standard blog is *micro-blogging*, where individuals will post very short news of their activities, or a commentary on events as they happen. Micro-blogging is usually associated with mobile technologies, but you will also encounter its equivalent in the status update which is common on social networking sites. An educational application for micro-blogging is yet to emerge, although there is probably scope for using it for peer support or keeping in touch while on field work.

> For two short *Common Craft* video clips on how blogs and Twitter are used for sharing news, visit the website to view a free evaluation video.
>
> http://www.commoncraft.com/blogs; http://www.commoncraft.com/twitter

Finally, some courses make use of *web conferencing* with distance or part-time students. These tools support speech and sometimes video over the Internet, together with access to a shared whiteboard for viewing presentations, images, web pages or graphs.

HOW COMMUNICATION TOOLS ARE USED FOR STUDY

Keeping in touch

One of the advantages of using online communication tools for study is that they offer plenty of opportunity for keeping in touch with fellow students and your tutors. That might begin even before you start your course, when there are opportunities to 'meet' students who have done the course, and to get some idea of what it might be like.

> Full-time students who apply to UK universities may encounter the *UCAS* website which has a wide range of online groups that you can join in order to meet fellow prospective students and chat about courses, or perhaps the stresses of coping with living away from home, finding a part-time job, student accommodation and so on.
>
> http://www.ucas.ac.uk

Some students like to maintain online contact with fellow students who have common interests and hobbies, using social networking or online chat. Both options can be a useful way to share information, talk about the course, stress, studying, or just life in general. This is especially helpful if you are studying away from campus and have few opportunities to join the clubs and societies which campus-based students enjoy.

I noticed with the last module that we gravitated towards chatting to others in similar home circumstances or with the same educational difficulties, e.g., mums with young children, mature students returning to study after decades out, people in demanding jobs trying to find time after work to bury their head in the books, folk with very little computer skills, people lagging behind, etc. As a result, if I was going to recommend anything at this stage, it would be to find people facing similar problems and discover that you are not alone!

Figure 6.1   Meeting students with similar interests

> *Facebook*, *BeBo* and *MySpace* are well known social networking sites, but there are others: *Elgg* is an open source tool which is often used for education, but you do need your own server to run it. *Ning* is another social networking site, which is straightforward to join.
>
> http://elgg.org; http://www.ning.com

Peer support groups

Online peer support groups may also be organised by your university or college, using either a forum, a community area on the VLE or social networking site. Cecily had signed up to a course, and decided to join a self-help group which was organised for the first few weeks of her course. The group was hosted by two students who had done the same course in the previous year, so they were able to tell the new students what it felt like, and help them to organise themselves for study. She was pleased that she had joined the group:

> *This forum's been great to help get rid of nerves … Everyone was extremely helpful and everyone was very enthusiastic. Some of the discussions that we had really helped to show how much everyone know about the subject already just from everyday life, and it was good to share ideas and points of view.*

Re: Introductions

Maria Thomas – 2 Sept, 06:00

By the way, as I am Spanish, I have been following the Spanish basketball team. The final against the USA was the best game of basketball that I have ever watched. In the end the best team (of course, the USA) won, but the game was an example of how healthy competition can make both teams perform at their highest levels.
Maria

Show parent Read by Edit Delete Reply (quote)

Matthew Potter – 2 Sep, 11:00

Hi,

I wish I'd seen this match. It's dazzling when the very best in the world are competing at the top of their game.

All very best wishes, Matthew

Show parent Read by Edit Delete Reply (quote)

Annie Spalcek - 2 Sep, 11:40

Hi, Maria,

Hola! So pleased to hear that you are Spanish, as I am studying Spanish ATM - and I had such a good week in Santiago recently.

Saludos, Annie

Show parent Read by Edit Delete Reply (quote)

Maria Thomas – 2 Sept, 11.45

Hi Annie,

Glad to hear that you enjoyed Santiago. Did you get to see much of the place? All of my father's side of the family come from Santiago. I love the place!

Regards,

Maria

Show parent Read by Edit Delete Reply (quote)

Figure 6.2   Use of a forum for meeting fellow students

Course discussion groups

Once the course gets underway, you will often get the chance to join
discussion groups to discuss important, interesting, or even boring parts of
the course. Course forums can provide an opportunity to raise difficulties
or to talk about course-related experiences you might have had at school,
at work or in your community. You will often find that a core group
of lively individuals post most of the messages while a larger group of
students benefit from reading the contributions of others. You might enjoy
posting messages yourself, once you begin to see what the discussion is
about, but you can also learn by reading what others have written. Often
fellow students come up with new ways of looking at parts of the course,
or maybe resources which can be handy for understanding or illustrating
course concepts. Fergus really appreciated this, especially when he was
thinking about writing the next assignment:

> *Forums were a lot more than chat. There were quite an eye opener on
> how the others were handling their assignments. Useful for getting an
> understanding of the facts. Great for getting ideas and information from
> peers: generating ideas.*

Exams and revision

Discussion groups can provide much valued support and encouragement
before the exam: and particularly during the revision period when you
may appreciate all the help you can get. The online group might discuss
appropriate revision techniques, or good practice in answering exam
questions. It can provide a space for you to learn from the tutor or fellow
students and also to share your worries and concerns.

Rachel:

> *Has anyone got a good way of remembering how block 3 fits together? I'm
> absolutely dreading having to write about it. It's a complete jumble in my
> head*

Sheena:

> *Have you thought of doing some concept mapping? I use one every hour
> or so when I'm revising – it just helps to sort out what connects to where.
> There is free software you can get off the web.*

Collaborative coursework

On some courses students need to undertake collaborative coursework
with a small group. If online contributions are assessed the discussion

group is a lot busier than it might otherwise have been, because everyone knows that it is important to contribute. Jane really enjoyed her online group work:

I felt really focused, we had a sense of responsibility and were mutually supportive, I was surprised at the level of feeling. Because we were chatting to each other and balancing each others arguments, you had to change your opinion a bit. The forum worked brilliantly. There was lots of information and exchange of ideas. People were very forthcoming. We met at a tutorial at the start and discussed main themes. We posted scripts on the forum: this was useful in a way and gives you an idea of what others are thinking.

Online classes

Finally students who do not have the opportunity to attend tutorials in a classroom sometimes get the chance to join online classes using web conferencing, see Figure 6.3. Web conferencing allows students to join live meetings over the Internet, from their own computer. The software allows a group of students to talk to the tutor and other group members over the Internet, while sharing access to a common whiteboard for displaying presentation slides, pictures, drawings, maps or web pages, and sometimes to transmit video pictures of themselves as well.

You can use polling or hand-raising to indicate agreement or doubt, and often online chat, which might be the equivalent of whispering at the back of the class. It is as close as you can get to a classroom experience without the travel, but regrettably without the socialising afterwards. In these sessions the tutor might explain significant or difficult parts of the course, and you have a chance to ask questions when you do not follow what the tutor (or other students) are talking about. An added advantage is the chance to be able to look at diagrams or formulae on the whiteboard, as is often important in maths, or perhaps to try out screen sharing, where others can see what is on your screen. In languages courses the tool provides an opportunity to practise speaking skills. Whatever the course, it can be reassuring to hear a human voice if you are otherwise mostly studying on your own, and if you missed the session you can watch a recording later.

FINAL COMMENTS

We hope you can see that there are many ways to communicate for your study. Some of this communication is really very informal, and closer to the kind of conversation you might have when emailing or texting friends. At other times you will practise writing in the language of the course when you discuss topics with fellow students. Some online communication is

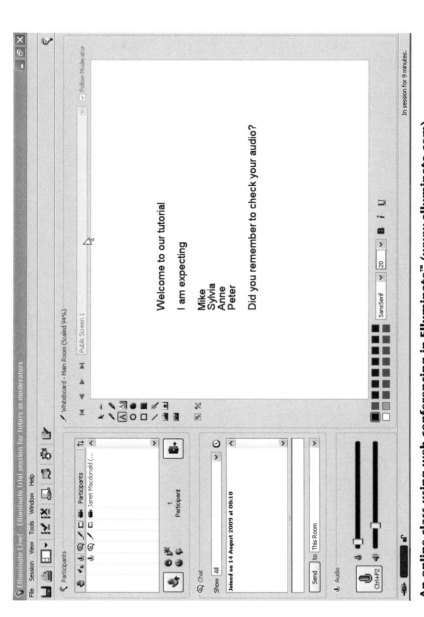

Figure 6.3   An online class using web conferencing in Elluminate™ (www.elluminate.com)

Source: Reproduced with kind permission from The Open University (UK).

very public and may be addressed to several hundred colleagues. Some is comment and opinion, with an altogether different flavour. Much involves written text, but you may also be speaking, or sharing pictures, video or audio clips. In the next chapter we give you some ideas on good practice in communicating for study.

7

Communicating and Community: A Survival Guide

Have been looking around to see what help I can get with this course from online groups, and what a relief, I found you lot! I didn't know how to write in the forum when I first started, but it's been great to see how others write about the course, and how that relates to people's lives. I'm beginning to see how I might contribute.

While communicating with groups of people is an important part of everyday life, it is not necessarily obvious how to do this appropriately for study. This chapter provides a survival guide on effective ways to communicate as part of a student group in college or university using online or mobile technologies.

51

COMMUNICATING WITH A GROUP

Before you can be successful in communicating for study purposes you need to have some idea of how it may feel, especially when you find yourself collaborating online with other students you may not know very well or have never met.

Try This

It is worth stopping to think about face-to-face discussion, and what makes it work: this is after all something which is familiar to all of us. You might try this exercise with your friends.

Watch a conversation in which one person is trying to explain something to the other. Try to write down exactly how that took place, what was said, and what you saw and felt.

In the course of a conversation which takes place face-to-face, some unconscious checking takes place which helps to establish what is known as *common ground*. This means that you watch for acknowledgement that the other person has understood what you are saying as you speak, and they will do the same for you. You might notice facial expressions such as an encouraging smile or blank look, and as a result you then repeat or rephrase what you have said to make the meaning clearer.

Conversations with a friend or colleague, or those which take place in a group usually have a kind of informal *turn taking*, in which you might need to watch for a space in the conversation and comment at an appropriate point. This all lends a buzz and sense of immediacy to discussion and often leads to unexpected twists and turns to the conversation.

Finally, the way in which your comments are received may often be related to previous *informal exchanges*. Informal exchanges help people to get to know each other, and can make the process of working together less threatening and altogether easier. It will certainly be important to put some effort into getting to know a bit about the people you are working with. While this is important in everyday life, it is even more essential when you are collaborating with a new or unfamiliar group of fellow students, with whom you are trying to make sense of some difficult concept or complete a group task set by your tutor.

Have you noticed how many of these comments on face-to-face communication refer to watching and listening? It is not surprising that the use of the written word to communicate tends to give everyone concerned a different kind of experience to being in a room together. If you cannot see the people you are communicating with, then you will need to seek other ways to establish common ground with them.

The story does not end here. There are many different reasons for communicating with a group, and you might find that certain tools are more effective in some circumstances than others.

We hope you can see that the various tools have different strengths, and if you are communicating using a text-based system like email you may need to be more conscious of effective communication than you would face-to-face or using the telephone, in order to make yourself understood.

GOOD PRACTICE GUIDELINES

In this section we give you some guidelines for text-based communication using a variety of tools. Very often there is a choice of tools which can serve a particular purpose and your choice will depend on what is in use

Try This

You might find it helpful to stop and think how effective various tools are for communicating in different contexts. You probably already have experience on which you can draw, such as using email or instant messaging with your friends and family, or with colleagues at work. We have introduced a few more tools to add to your collection. Why not try to complete this table by scoring each strategy for its strengths, using a scale 1–5 where 1=of little value; and 5=extremely valuable.

	Building confidence	Allowing time to think about a response	Brainstorming ideas	Understanding explanations	Communicating humour or sadness
face-to-face					
email					
phone conversation					
instant messaging					
sms					
forum					
audio					
social networking					
blog					

by your tutors and fellow students, what is readily available, as well as which tools you feel most comfortable and confident with.

Online discussion groups

Tools you might use

Discussion forum; social networking; personal profile; file-sharing sites

There will often be a variety of online groups available to you, each with a different character and set up for different reasons: we have shown you what some of those purposes might be in the last chapter. Before you write anything in a new online discussion group it is a good idea to familiarise yourself with the environment and perhaps read a few messages from other participants: that is rather like walking into a crowded room and looking around before you open your mouth. Look out for clues about the purposes of the group you join. Be aware that each group will have its own ways of writing: some will be for course discussion, and you might expect to be writing about course concepts, while others will be social groups for letting off steam, or talking about hobbies and wider interests. It is good to get a feel for how you will be expected to write.

How you derive benefit from an online discussion will depend on whether it is a group to which you are required to contribute or one which is entirely optional, but which is going to be useful for you to join. Whatever the choice, be aware that participating in online groups can be time consuming: if you are going to keep up with an online conversation you will need to read messages regularly, or you are likely to become overwhelmed. That might mean that you need to visit the site several times a day, but this depends on the size of the group and the liveliness of the discussion. In groups which are optional it is common for some students to post messages regularly while others prefer just to read: you will have to decide what works for you. You will soon recognise people in the group who post messages which are likely to be most useful, but above all do not believe everything you read! Online discussion groups are often used as a place to try out ideas, and sometimes even the writer does not really mean what they have written.

If you are used to writing emails then you will already have useful experience to draw on when you take part in a discussion group. The big difference is that you will be writing your message to a group which may include people you have never met, especially if you are studying at a distance. It is therefore a good idea to get to know a little about them and to share some information about yourself. If you have space on the VLE for your profile or a page on a social networking site, use it to share a bit of information about yourself: it can help to build bridges and gives the other students a sense of who you are. You might make use of photos or cartoons, or even short audio clips if you feel confident enough to do that.

I live in Birmingham and have a husband, one 13 year old son, one big mad dog, a part time job, and I last studied in college about 17 years ago. Really excited about starting this course, but still wondering what on earth I've let myself in for...

PS Anyone fancy a bit of dog walking while I'm busy studying?

Figure 7.1   Use of a profile to share information about yourself

Where files are large it is good practice to make use of a file-sharing site and to include a link to the site in your message rather than the file itself. This means that fellow students can choose whether or not to view or download your file. At the same time be aware of the information you choose to share with an unknown readership. While a profile site on a VLE will be available only to a restricted group of fellow students, many social networking sites have a much wider readership and you will need to use the site's privacy options carefully to restrict access to your personal information.

When you are ready to contribute a message to the discussion group, you will probably be hoping that what you write will be interesting for others to read. How will you tempt them to do so?

55

> ### *Try This*
>
> You might have noticed messages from a fellow student which you enjoyed reading: why not make a list of the reasons for this? Here are some thoughts we have, but you might feel differently:
>
>   *'I can see where she is coming from.'*
>   *'He really did a lot of work on this.'*
>   *'This is someone I would really get along with if I met them.'*
>   *'He doesn't make me feel stupid.'*
>   *'She uses a friendly tone and wants to know what others think.'*

When writing in a discussion group it is common to use a conversational tone, and to write as you would speak. At the same time you might wish to experiment in using some of the academic terms and ways of writing used in your course: it can be a good opportunity to practise being an apprentice in your field. It is also helpful to keep your message short and concise, making sure the title is meaningful so that others can decide immediately if it is something they would be interested in reading. Remember that you are taking part in a group discussion, rather than giving a speech on a podium. This means that it makes sense to refer to another student's views where they are relevant, and perhaps to leave the door open for others to contribute, by sometimes finishing your message with an open question.

Whose messages would you rather read: Simon's or Cynthia's?

Simon:

> *Frankly I think the concept of 'moral panic' is pretty obvious and really not difficult to grapple with, so I don't know what the fuss is about. I usually find in these courses that those of us with the intelligence to follow the instructions and get the assignments in on time have little use for this kind of rambling discussion.*

Cynthia:

> *I was interested in what Selina was saying and so I did some searching on moral panics today and I threw up a number of interesting sites. Here's one you might be interested in as it explains in some depth why the writer believes that the HIV issue was a moral panic. If you come across other examples I'd really like to hear from you.*

You may already be aware of those embarrassing times when you sent messages which were not read quite the way you had intended. The sad fact is that irony or cynicism and even humour can be difficult to communicate and can easily be misinterpreted, especially if you do not know the person who wrote the message. If you cannot see the people you are communicating with, it is a good idea to say how you feel, or make occasional use of emoticons.

> *I agree/disagree*
> *I'm confused*
> *I feel strongly about this*
> *I'm finding this very interesting*

Lastly, stop and think: we have all posted messages which we later regret.

Most forum messages are short, but sometimes you might need to send a longer message, in which case you might consider creating a document and sending it as an attachment to your message. If you have a large file to share, for example pictures or an audio or video clip, then you could save them to a file-sharing site and give people a link.

Quick tips: online discussion groups (forums, social networking)

- Find out the purpose of the group and note how others write;
- be ready to participate regularly;
- watch your time;
- do not believe everything you read;
- introduce yourself with a little information about your background or interests;
- write as you speak, and keep your message concise with a meaningful title;
- be ready to respond to others, taking part in the discussion;
- be explicit about your feelings so it is clear what you are communicating;
- be considerate to other group members;
- think before you send;
- use file attachments or links to other sites for longer messages or large files.

57

Online publishing

Tools you might use

Blogs

In the last chapter we referred to the use of blogs in the context of publishing news, often with a personal commentary. We explained that blogs are generally used for publishing a monologue rather than for a conversation with others, and therefore the way you write might be rather different than it would be in a discussion group because you are less likely to be building on, or responding to, other messages. At the same time, there is an expectation that you will have an audience of people who have a choice whether to read your blog or not. They may even choose to comment on, or to link to your blog so that they receive regular updates. It is therefore in your best interest to write in a way which will be attractive or interesting for people to read, and so the comments made in the last section together with much of the advice on readability is as applicable to blogs as it is to online discussion groups. Basically the way you write your blog should suit the purpose of the blog and its readership.

Because readers may not wish to read every entry in your blog, it is helpful to give an informative title to each entry and to get into the habit of tagging your entries with key words and phrases: this is a way of coding entries by subject, and can help people who are searching for blogs with an interest in common with their own, as the tags will be picked up by search engines.

Try This

Use the blog search engine *Technorati* to search for a subject you are interested in. You will see that you are given the option of searching for individual blog entries, or alternatively for complete blogs.

http://technorati.com/

(All web links are listed at the back of the book, and on our book website at: http://sites.google.com/site/learnonlinegroup/).

Quick tips: online publishing (blogs)

- Think about the audience and communicate in a way which fits the purpose of your blog and the people who you hope will read it;
- use tags to describe the content;
- upload pictures or multimedia to enhance the blog;
- link to related blogs if you like.

Socialising and peer support

Tools you might use

Instant messaging; online chat; SMS; micro blogs; social networking

A range of technologies are commonly in use for everyday social contact, and they are also useful for keeping in touch at college or university. Instant messaging or online chat can be effective for short informal sessions with fellow students and SMS text is useful for quick queries.

What was the title of that essay again?

Dunno I lost the piece of paper.

In terms of good practice, it is really up to you to decide how you want to use these tools in an educational context, as it is simply an extension of what takes place in day-to-day life.

If you have a *Facebook* account it could be worth checking to see whether there are active peer support groups for your course or in your geographical area.

http://www.Facebook.com

If you plan to meet with fellow students or your tutor for a short web chat session then the following guidelines may be helpful. Write in short sections, and break up longer statements with three dots, to show that there is another message to follow. If you are part of a group there is often a danger that conversation will become anarchic, with everyone posting at once and with overlapping comments. One of your group may be chosen to act as Chair to control the flow of conversation, just so that it does not get too confusing. You may be asked to use certain conventions such as sending '!' in a message or clicking on a raised hand icon to let the Chair know you have something to say, then waiting for a signal from the Chair such as 'GA' (Go Ahead), which gives you permission to contribute.

Micro-blogging allows you to send short messages to let others know what you are doing or thinking at different times of the day, and you can also choose to 'follow' other people so that you receive automatic updates from them on your computer or mobile phone. These can be useful or simply distracting, depending on how you decide to use this tool and which people you choose to follow. You might like to find out if any experts in your area of study are micro-bloggers and decide to become one of their followers.

Quick tips: socialising and peer support (web chat, social networking, micro-blogs)

- For online chat, organise a suitable time to meet the group online;
- write in short sections of text;
- establish turn taking rules before you start;
- identify a Chair if necessary;
- on social networking sites, join relevant student support groups;
- make sure you have set appropriate privacy options to control who can view your personal details;
- when micro-blogging, consider how the messages you send and the responses you receive from others might benefit your learning.

The online classroom

Tools you might use

Web conferencing

While web conferencing provides a wonderful opportunity to meet in a virtual classroom for those who are unable to attend a campus, the experience is still very different from sharing a classroom with fellow students, and the following guidelines outline a few ideas on best practice to make a session work well.

You will probably receive an invitation from your tutor to join one of these sessions at a fixed time, so there is an opportunity to plan ahead a little. In particular, before the session starts make sure that you have the right equipment: you will need a headset with microphone, together with a webcam if you are video conferencing. Check your audio levels, ensure you can hear and be heard, and make sure your camera is working, if you need one. If you are joining from work then you need to make sure that the system works and is not hampered by institutional firewalls. It is a good idea to ensure you will not be disturbed: hang a notice on your door and consider turning off email, instant messaging and games on your computer so that you can concentrate on the session.

You might find that these conferencing sessions are quite hard work, and it takes some practice to become familiar with the tool before you can relax a little and just concentrate on what is being discussed. The comments we have already made about working with an unseen group still apply in web conferencing, even though the use of video gives you some clue about fellow participants. People feel more at ease when they know a little about the fellow students in their group, so you need to devote some effort to helping that to work. Use of an online profile to share some information about yourself can help. Once the session starts be ready to introduce yourself. Beyond giving your name, a little information perhaps explaining where you are calling from (whether a cupboard under stairs at home, library or deserted office) can help to make the contact a little easier. As the discussion proceeds you will gain a picture of the group participants, and this is often supported by the software which commonly gives you a list of participants, and indicates who is speaking.

As you contribute to the session be aware that your facial expression and the way you are feeling can influence the tone of your voice. You would be surprised how much of this is conveyed with audio. So speak to the group just as you would to someone in the room. Be aware that silences can be misinterpreted, and you may need to be open about how you feel. Regularly acknowledge that you are listening to contributions from your fellow students, even if you do not have anything more substantive to say. Of course with video you can nod or smile. When you use audio, be ready to use polling or feedback buttons to show the tutor you are still online, and listening intently.

In web conferencing only one person can speak at a time, and this makes a conversation rather more formal than it might otherwise be.

You may need to let the tutor know you wish to speak: with some applications, this is achieved by clicking on a raised hand icon. Many web conferencing systems have a whiteboard for sharing diagrams or other visual material, or perhaps for sharing links to interesting websites. Resist the temptation to doodle or scribble on it, unless you are invited to do so.

Finally, if you missed the session altogether, fell asleep halfway through or simply wish to go over the session again for revision purposes, you may benefit from a recording of the session when it is finished. Make use of the transcript if there is one: it can be a useful way of running through important points and checking your understanding. And if you plan to snooze through the session, check first that there will be a recording, and that your microphone and webcam are switched off.

Quick tips: online classrooms (web conferencing)

- Check audio levels and camera settings before the session;
- ensure you will be undisturbed;
- turn off other software on your computer;
- be ready to introduce yourself;
- be aware of the tone of your voice;
- regularly acknowledge contributions by using polling or hand raising;
- make use of the transcript to run through important points afterwards.

61

Face-to-face contact

If you have limited opportunities to visit the campus or otherwise to meet your fellow students and tutor during your course of study, make the most of them when they occur. Think carefully about where you benefit: there might be particular parts of the course which you find difficult to understand and for which you need an explanation by meeting up with your tutor. Perhaps it is important to see what the staff look like, and to meet your fellow students and make a few friends, especially at the start of the course. Sometimes it can be quite supportive to meet folk who struggle with the same parts of the course as you do yourself: or to realise that students come from a wide variety of backgrounds and may see the course rather differently than you do yourself. Such issues are often easier to deal with face-to-face than they are online, as Sabine explains:

Although the online group was brilliant it was really reassuring to see people face-to-face and to hear directly how everyone else felt the same as I did.

FINAL COMMENTS

We have described good practice in communicating within a community of students. You will have seen that there is often a choice of applications which can be used for a particular purpose, and that will depend on what is most readily available to the group. Probably the most important thing you need to remember from this chapter is how important it is to be aware of the purpose of your group communication, and to be sensitive to the interests and values of your readers, and what that means for an acceptable way of writing. We continue in the next chapter to describe an activity which is probably as common for students as communicating: that is 'Searching and researching'.

8 Searching and Researching

I'm really happy with a choice of resources… if a route is more beneficial to me, I will follow it. I much prefer the freedom to do a bit of detective work… it also improves my study skills. It really keeps interest high, it helps having different media and different resources to access. I like the choice and the variation, not being bogged down in one book. I prefer to read on screen, you can make the type large, and scrolling down is lazier than turning a page.

Very few of you, if any, will not have used web resources. Perhaps you have looked for a map of an area where you want to go on holiday, and then booked your flights online. Maybe you wanted to check what was coming up on TV, or bought an outfit for a party next week. You may have downloaded a recording of a radio or TV programme which you missed, or checked on the weather forecast, or saw whether your mother's train was running on time, and when you needed to go to the station to meet her. If you got lost on the way to the station you may have used your mobile to check for directions and look up the best route.

You may be wondering how much of this is relevant to study in a university or college, or to what extent the tools you use already might help you. This chapter describes the tools you may encounter and shows how digital resources can support your study. We concentrate here on two areas: resource-based study where the course expects you to undertake independent searching, or alternatively where you decide to make use of additional web resources which are not a core part of course content but which you feel will enhance your study. For more about the use of technologies for studying core course content we refer you to Chapter 4 on 'Listening, reading and sense-making'.

THE GROWTH AND IMPACT OF WEB RESOURCES

In recent years, the Internet has enabled a dramatic expansion of the quantity and range of web resources. Educational resources which were once only available to those who could visit libraries or museums have become available on the web. These resources include not only text but also multimedia, and this chapter describes a few examples. In addition, since anyone can publish on social networking sites there has been an enormous rise in what is known as 'user-generated content'. For example, where TV and newspapers used once to distribute news for readers to digest, they now receive regular input in the form of pictures from mobile phones or commentary in blogs. In fact the person in the street is actively contributing to and commenting on the news, and this principle extends to many aspects of life.

Whether user-generated content is appropriate to study at college or university will depend on your course. Traditionally higher education courses encourage the use of peer-reviewed content, which has been written by academics and then rigorously reviewed by colleagues so that it is effectively 'kitemarked' as being of a scholarly and reliable standard, before it reaches the reader. In contrast, much user-generated content on the web is rated by its readers for popularity or relevance for a particular purpose, whether that is by a five star rating, or by the number of micro-blog posts which refer to it, or perhaps by the number of links to the site which are picked up by social bookmarking or a search engine. It is important to be aware of the distinction between user-generated content and scholarly or official sources, and particularly to be alive to the assessment requirements of the course you are studying because that will define what is acceptable practice on your course.

TOOLS FOR SEARCHING AND RESEARCHING

Tools you might use

Web browser; search engines; social bookmarking; web feeds; e-portfolios

Many of the online tools which you probably encounter in everyday life are useful to you when you set out to do some searching for study purposes. The most common is the *web browser*, which might be Internet Explorer or a host of alternatives which work just as well, or even better.

Opera, Apple Safari, Mozilla Firefox and *Google Chrome* are web browsers which are freely available on the web, and provide an alternative to using *Internet Explorer*.

http://www.opera.com/; http://www.mozilla-europe.org/en/firefox/

(All web links are listed at the back of the book, and on our book website at: http://sites.google.com/site/learnonlinegroup/).

The browser allows you to display resources in web pages which may contain text or multimedia. Links in the web page lead to further pages within the same document, or to different websites. Each web page has its own address or URL (Uniform Resource Locator) which you can type or copy into the address bar at the top of the screen. The link which is given in the box on this page is an example of a URL. Browsers have an in-built bookmarking facility which allows you to save the web links of sites you wish to return to, but this has limitations because they are only saved on the computer you are using at the time. They also include feed readers or aggregators which collect regularly updated content from selected news websites, blogs or podcasts, and present them in one place so that you have news which is tailored to your needs.

Micro-browsers do the same job as browsers, but on mobile devices. However most people use mobile devices for quick checking of facts rather than lengthy reading material, because their small screens make reading hard work.

Web browsers have a search bar in which you can type in the terms you wish to look for, using your preferred *search engine*. Search engines allow you to search the web with your browser. You simply type in a key words or phrases and the search engine displays a list of sites of varying relevance. There are many search engines to choose from, each with its own characteristics.

Two of the most commonly used search engines are *Google* and *Google Scholar* (for academic purposes).

http://www.google.com; http://scholar.google.co.uk/

In the course of your study you are likely to collect large numbers of web links which are often long and notoriously easy to forget, so the business of finding a website can be frustrating, even if you have been there before. It is often useful to keep a record of the web address when you find sites of interest, so that you can visit again. We have mentioned that browsers have bookmarking facilities which allow you to do this. Some students make use of a specialist tool which records and manages citations of academic papers, books and journals which they wish to refer to in essays and reports.

Documentit is one example of a tool for recording and managing citations, and helping students to learn correct referencing. Free download for students.

http://www.documentit.co.uk/

An alternative is *social bookmarking:* websites where you can store web links together with a note of their content, the date when you visited the site and some keywords or 'tags' to describe the subject matter. This means that provided you have online access you can access your links wherever you are, regardless of which computer or mobile device you are using. By searching your collection of links using tags you can simply retrieve the links which are relevant to a particular purpose.

For a short video clip on how social bookmarking works, visit the *Common Craft* website to view a free evaluation copy.

http://www.commoncraft.com/bookmarking-plain-english

The social bookmarking website also allows you to share your tags with colleagues, hence the term *social* bookmarking: this means you can see what links others have stored against the same tags. Some sites allow ratings, so that you can rank how helpful you found the site and see how helpful others found it to be. That means your social bookmarking site works like a search engine, helping you to locate relevant sites which have been rated by other users. In fact some people find that this user-generated rating is more useful than that produced automatically by a search engine, but that really depends on the extent to which your interests coincide with the interests of others and of course the extent to which you trust their judgement.

If you need to keep up to date with news from a variety of online resources commonly including blogs, news websites or podcasts, then you may well find that *web feeds* can be useful to you. Web or news feeds are web files which can collect updated content by theme from a variety of sites, which means the subscriber can receive regular updates without having to visit several sites on a regular basis. Web feeds are read using a feed reader on your computer or mobile device. Commonly on sites which offer a web feed, you will see the icon shown in Figure 8.1.

By clicking on the icon, you can choose to subscribe to updates as they appear. All you need to do then is to remember to check them regularly, and some people do

Figure 8.1 Really Simple Syndication (RSS) web feed icon

so every day, just as they might pick up the newspaper. Martin does this on the train:

> *I use my iPhone to download articles from papers I might be interested in from web feeds. I check it all on the train to work.*

In fact, some people prefer to do this rather than buying a newspaper, since it allows them to concentrate on the articles particularly of interest from a wide variety of sources, and of course it saves paper. If the feed contains podcasts you have the option of listening to them on your computer, or transferring them to a mobile device for a more convenient listening time.

For a short video clip on how RSS is used for reading websites, visit the *Common Craft* website to view a free evaluation copy.

http://www.commoncraft.com/rss_plain_english

ONLINE RESOURCES WHICH CAN HELP YOUR STUDY 67

The web is a source of many rich and varied resources which can be useful and relevant for study. For most students the first port of call is the tutor who will often provide guidance on resources which they know will be particularly valuable to your coursework. Such resource lists can often enhance and broaden your understanding of the course, and ensure that you are introduced to appropriate resources. We can simply show you some of the exciting possibilities. Not all of these sites are free and some will need to be accessed through your institution's library.

User-generated content

When looking for basic background information on a topic many people will turn to Wikipedia: a very good example of user-generated content. Because this is a resource which can be contributed to by anyone it is not always reliable, although the fact that entries may be continually amended can help to moderate extreme cases of misleading information.

Wikipedia is the most well known of the Wikimedia projects which provide free wiki-based content on a wide variety of areas including *Wikispecies, Wikiquote, Wikiversity.*

http://www.wikipedia.org; http://www.wikimedia.org

Official sources

Be aware that there are many other resources which can provide reliable information of relevance to study at university or college: we give you a few examples here.

Oxford Reference contains reliable facts, figures and definitions from 175+ Oxford reference titles.

http://www.oxfordreference.com

On some courses you may need to make use of original sources such as the letters of a writer, or perhaps official government statistics.

The publication hub for *UK National Statistics* provides access to government statistics on a wide variety of areas including business and energy, health and social care, travel and transport.

http://www.statistics.gov.uk/hub/

A wide range of multimedia resources has become available on the web, so you could locate a film clip, or some pictures from an exhibition or museum.

SCRAN is one of the largest educational online services in the UK. Sponsored by the Royal Commission on the Ancient and Historical Monuments of Scotland, it is a database of digital materials including images and movies on culture and world heritage from the archives of museums and galleries. Visitors can view thumbnail images free; the full image is available to subscribers.

http://www.scran.ac.uk

The *British Library sound recordings* collection contains over 1500 recordings of UK dialects, british wildlife and classical music.

http://sounds.bl.uk

In addition, many topical radio programmes can be downloaded from the broadcaster's website and listened to for a limited amount of time after they have been broadcast. If there is a particular series of broadcasts which are relevant to your area of study, you may wish to subscribe to podcasts of the full series.

Open educational content

You may encounter the term *open educational content*, used to describe educational material which is used as part of formal courses, but which is also freely available on the web for self-study purposes. The material is commonly available under Creative Commons licensing, which means that anyone may use the material, provided they attribute the source when it is used in written work. That means citing the author and where the material has been found.

OpenLearn is one of the world's largest repositories of open content course material. It contains learning materials and free use of communication tools from Open University (UK) courses.

http://www.open.ac.uk/openlearn

Both iTunesU and YouTube have a range of academic lectures and videos from various universities which are available for public use. Be aware that both sites also host a wide range of resources which we would categorise as user generated and therefore to be used with care.

Library and peer-reviewed resources

We could not leave this section without pointing you to your institution's library. The library is traditionally the place where you can go to source material for written work. In addition to paper resources most libraries provide access to a wide variety of online resources and some also make use of social bookmarking to indicate resources which are popular with other readers. Perhaps most importantly they are staffed by expert subject librarians, whose job involves helping people to find relevant resources. The key is probably to be ready to use a variety of sources, as Saleem explains:

> *I found the course book really provided a great introduction to the subject. Then I read a few journal papers which were quite hard going but they had the information and they are peer reviewed so you know it's the right sort of quality. And finally I did a bit of a web search just to illustrate some of the issues.*

The library provides access to scholarly journals which are valued by students on some courses because they are generally 'peer reviewed'. This means that they have been scrutinised and commented upon by fellow academics, which gives them extra credibility. Textbooks may also be available as e-books, which can be particularly valuable where they are set books.

You can also ask your librarians about specialised *Subject Gateways* which allow you to browse a range of online resources which have been organised and classified by subject experts. Most academic libraries will provide links to these on their websites.

Google books is a service which allows you to search for books online. Many books, including out-of-print editions are available in full text, while for other books you can search book contents or sample chapters.

www.books.google.co.uk

FINAL COMMENTS

We hope we have whetted your appetite for searching web resources and for trying out a range of tools to find them. It is important to know about user-generated content, and to recognise how it is different from content produced by official sources or peer-reviewed papers. There can be difficulties in using user-generated content for academic work, but that depends on your course. In the end, you need to be guided by your tutor and librarians. In the next chapter we provide some pointers to good practice in searching and researching for study.

9 Searching and Researching: A Survival Guide

I feel quite confident about finding material on the web now. There's a lot of stuff, and there's lots I don't bother with. To begin with I was not selective enough, not good at getting the gist. In the early stages I printed out whole articles, then I learnt to find relevant paragraphs. I don't know if I've got better at sorting through a lot of material. It is a matter of narrowing down the search, and trying alternative strategies. But I still have to exert a great deal of self-control or I tend to read too much.

One of the main strengths of the Internet is that anyone can make a resource available to anyone else, anywhere in the world. However this is also one of its main weaknesses. Making the most of online resources is an essential feature of studying so it is important to know what is involved and to think about the opportunities and challenges. This chapter gives you some tips on searching for and making effective use of online resources. It also tells you about good practice when using online resources for academic study and it covers a very important issue: how to avoid plagiarism.

ONLINE SEARCHING AND HIGHER EDUCATION

As a student, you have new and exciting possibilities for study because of online web resources. Instead of waiting to be told what to learn you can search and research on your own initiative, in order to enhance your coursework. Many courses are designed with projects where you are expected to research a topic in some depth: this is called resource-based or sometimes project-based learning. Searching and researching can be challenging because you need to develop a critical and questioning approach to the resources you find, but this comes with practice. It is no good believing everything you read. In this context, your university or college may refer to information literacy: that is the ability to find and use multiple resources effectively and appropriately.

How We Learn 5

It takes time and practice to develop independence and self-direction as a learner. A classic study charted the development of American college students as they learnt the practice of critical thinking over the years of their life at college. To start with the students saw the world, or what they were reading as either right or wrong, and the researchers called this attitude dualism. At the end of their time at college they arrived at what the researchers called relativism where they were able to appreciate diversity in points of view and had developed a more critical approach to their reading.

Source: Perry, W. (1970).

We conclude that, at best, if you make use of additional online resources for study, it can deepen your understanding and provide good examples of course concepts. At worst it can lead to plagiarism and the misuse of resources.

WARNING: PLAGIARISM!

We are going to start with a warning. If you are able to search the web with Google, have found Wikipedia and know how to cut and paste bits of text from one source to another, you might be thinking that it is going to be pretty straightforward to produce written work for your tutor which looks good and takes very little time to produce. Think again! Louise learnt her lesson the hard way:

> *I failed my first assignment which I thought looked pretty good, but my tutor seemed to think otherwise. I was criticised for plagiarism which I hadn't even thought about. I thought I had some good stuff, but apparently some of it was from unreliable sources. I find it very difficult to be selective in picking out what is really important from such a mass of possibilities. So much of this stuff you see on the web looks like it's written by experts so how could I write any better as a student? I suppose it's a case of adapting to computer-based learning, and knowing how to adapt.*

You do need a good understanding of what is meant by plagiarism and how to avoid it if you want to do well in your studies. Plagiarism is often simply defined as passing off someone else's work as your own. Many students can be guilty of plagiarism through lack of confidence in their ability to express themselves well. Some students run into difficulties with plagiarism because of poor time management. They started their coursework at the last minute and are desperately trying to produce a polished piece of work in a few hours. You may find writing especially difficult if you are not studying in your preferred language because you are not only dealing with a less familiar language, but also often a new set of expectations on how you should write.

> You might be interested to listen to a video clip of students' comments on *plagiarism*, produced by the UK Higher Education Academy.
>
> http://www.heacademy.ac.uk/resources/ then search for student views plagiarism.
>
> (All web links are listed at the back of the book, and on our book website at: http://sites.google.com/site/learnonlinegroup/).

Whatever the reasons for it, colleges and universities are increasingly concerned about plagiarism, and you should be aware of it too. Some institutions now use automated plagiarism detection systems, in which either tutors or students submit their written work in electronic form to a detection facility. This compares your work against electronic sources and produces an originality report, so if your written work looks too much like a source on the Internet, or shows too many similarities to the work of a fellow student, the system will identify the overlaps. It is obviously much less embarrassing to avoid this situation before it occurs, and the advice which follows is worth taking to heart.

73

> To see the kind of checking undertaken by detection systems have a look at the *Turnitin* site
>
> http://turnitin.com/static/popups/sample_report.html

GOOD PRACTICE GUIDELINES

The most common time when students decide they need to search for information and resources is just before they need to write an assignment. Sadly it is often also when they have left the assignment until the last minute and find themselves hard pressed to produce their written work on time. It is a fact that being short of time is not a great start to becoming an effective searcher and can often lead to a choice of the wrong sources, for the wrong reasons. Many students in these circumstances will turn to Google and Wikipedia because it is easy to do so, but often with disappointing results. We would like to show you the alternatives.

When you first start out in your studies you will probably be given guidance from your tutor on when and where you need to seek out further resources for written work. You will be given a reading list for your course which is likely to include printed books and journals as well as links to useful websites and online resources. With so much information freely available over the Internet there is a strong temptation to limit your reading to what is easiest to find online without going to the effort of visiting a library or bookshop. It is useful to consider the practicalities of purchasing or borrowing the essential books for your course, and worth recognising that some online resources may not be an adequate replacement. As Nigel comments:

> *Nowadays there's more of a tendency to rely on the computer, whereas I will use a computer, but realise it's a tool, not the be all and end all, and I also go and get books. I think that makes a big difference to my reports.*

A reading list can save a lot of time and can help you to understand the types of information which you are required to read for your course. Then if you choose to do some independent searching, you can at least look for material with a similar style and audience to the material on your reading list. Remember that when you are studying there is still plenty of relevant material which exists in paper form, and cannot be found on the web.

When you are undertaking independent project work you are more likely to be given a free rein, and may be expected to do extensive searching for a variety of resources. You will be well equipped for this stage if you have developed good practice in investigating from the start of your course of study.

In this section we give you some guidelines for searching and researching using a variety of online tools.

Deciding on your search strategy

Tools you might use

Web browser; search engines; social bookmarking

You may have found that trawling through websites can become an entertainment in itself. It is so easy to move between sites and to jump between one subject and the next, that you can forget why you went online in the first place. So get focused!

Try This

You might find it helpful to write yourself a list before you start searching:
- what do I already know about the subject (in outline)?
- where are the gaps, and what do I need to find out?
- what do I need to understand better?

Thinking about the gaps in this way helps to focus the mind and will help you to concentrate your time in searching only for what you really need for your written work. A well-prepared search strategy will simplify your search and help you to avoid accessing irrelevant resources. Some preparatory work will save a considerable amount of time and frustration.

Search engines are a very easy way to search for information on the web, and what you find may be a lot more than you need. You also need to be aware that your choice of search engine will determine what you find, indeed the use of one search engine may not cover the relevant type of resource. While Google and Google Scholar are among the most popular search engines in use, there are a number of specialised search engines. The subject librarians within your institution will be able to help you with accessing scholarly databases which are especially targeted to your own subject area and which often require specialised search techniques.

Different search engines will retrieve different lists of sites. Be aware that for some search engines the sites which appear at the top of a search list will be those to which there are most links, so the search list acts as a measure of the popularity of the sites. Popularity might not necessarily mean quality, or relevance to your purpose in searching the web, although it could mean both. Other search engines allow businesses to pay for their website or resource to be favourably listed and ranked. This means that the results you get may not be as useful and helpful to you as you would wish.

Try This

Metacrawler is a search engine which gathers hits across several search engines.

Use *Metacrawler* to search for the term 'social bookmarking'.

Each entry shows you which search engine has located it.

You can see how the different search engines will generate different hits.

http://www.metacrawler.com

Fallon likes to use a search engine as a way of getting her brain in gear and seeing what is available on the subject:

> *What I usually do when I have an assignment to write is I type the words from the assignment title into a search engine. It's quite a good way of just*

scoping the territory, seeing the range of stuff which it turns up. Then I can just concentrate on the relevant areas and do some more searching.

Using relevant keywords is an important part of searching for information. Some common words will return far too many results or 'hits', and you may need to limit your search by adding some additional words which will narrow down the number of sites found. Conversely, if your search returns a disappointing number of results, you may need to try again with other keywords which have a similar meaning or restrict your search to certain countries or dates. Most search engines have advanced features which will help you to do this.

The use of a social bookmarking site can provide an additional approach to using a search engine. If you are working collaboratively with a group of students you could arrange to share sites you have found.

Try This

- Sign up for an account with a social bookmarking site.
- Agree with a group of your fellow students to use the same site.
- You will be prompted to install bookmarking buttons on your browser.
- When you find a useful website, save the link to your site.
- Add tags to describe the content.
- Agree with your group to use certain common tags.
- Give each link a rating if you like.
- Using your tags search for useful sites you have saved.
- Have a look to see what sites your fellow students have saved against the same tags.
- See what rating they gave for their links.

Judging usefulness and relevance

Tools you might use

Web browser; search engines

Having decided what you are looking for and chosen a number of resources, you also need to think about types of information. Web resources are written for all sorts of reasons and a wide variety of purposes and readerships. You will need to make decisions about the reliability of the information you find. The web has many sites which are out of date, or those which reflect one person's opinion, some based on fact and others on fabrication, while many are designed to present information in a way which sells a particular product.

Try This

It is important to be wary of the quality of Internet resources. Information that you find online may be out of date, incorrect, incomplete or biased. You should evaluate the quality of the resources you find online in the same way that you would evaluate other sources of information. There are simple questions which can help you to decide whether the site you have visited is likely to be valuable for your coursework.

Start by asking yourself:
- who wrote it?
- who published it?
- for whom and why?
- when was it created?
- are there copyright restrictions?

Before you even open a website, you can establish very quickly whether it is likely to be useful for your purpose: just look at the web address. This will give you some vital clues, on *how*, *where* and for *whom* it was produced. For example, if you look at the following web address it gives you many clues as to who published the document, how, for whom and why.

http://www.nationalarchives.gov.uk/cabinetpapers/

How? http:// (hypertext transfer protocol) – this is the method used to access the website.

Where? nationalarchives.gov.uk – the information is stored on the National Archives computer. The letters gov. and uk. tell you that this is a government organisation, situated in the UK.

What? cabinetpapers – this tells you what information has been stored. In this case it is past cabinet papers.

You will find more on the common codes used in web links by turning to Appendix B.

Try This

Try searching for 'plagiarism' using a search engine. By looking at the web address see if you can work out which sites are from universities or colleges, and which are from commercial providers who might wish to sell you something. The clues are there if you look carefully.

Having looked at the web address and decided that the site is worth looking at further, what else do you look for on the site, and how do you decided it will be suitable? You could use the PROMPT checklist.

Evaluating information: PROMPT

- **P**resentation
  Is the information clearly communicated?
  Look at language, layout, structure, and so on.
- **R**elevance
  Does the information match the needs of the searcher?
  Look at the introduction or overview. What is it mainly about?
- **O**bjectivity
  Is the author's position of interest made clear?
  Look for an introduction or overview. Do the writers state their position on the issue? Is the language emotive? Are there hidden, vested interests?
- **M**ethod (research reports only)
  Is it clear how the data was collected?
  Were the methods appropriate? Do you trust it?
- **P**rovenance
  Is it clear where the information has come from?
  Can you identify the authors or organisations? How was it published?
- **T**imeliness
  Is it clear when the information was produced?
  Does the date of the information meet your requirements? Is it obsolete?

Source: Reproduced from SAFARI (Skills in Accessing, Finding and Reviewing Information; http://www.open.ac.uk/safari) with kind permission from The Open University, UK.

Quick tips: search strategies and relevance (web browser; search engines; social bookmarking)

- Be guided by your course reading list and your tutor;
- allow yourself time to do your searching properly;
- think about the gaps in your knowledge of the topic and what you need to find out;
- consider alternatives to Google or Wikipedia;
- get wise about search engines;
- choose relevant types of information for your study;
- check out the source of information from the web address;
- bookmark your weblinks, share them if you wish;
- develop a critical approach to the resources you find: do not believe everything you read;
- remember the course books;
- get help from the library and librarians.

Using the information retrieved

Tools you might use

Word processor; web browser; social bookmarking

There are three very important skills which you need if you intend to make effective use of online resources for study. They are easy to remember because they follow the alphabet:

Paraphrasing and summarising
Quoting
Referencing

Paraphrasing means describing someone else's written work using your own words, and writing in your own style. You may also need to summarise, which means noting the most important points and then writing it in your own words. Both paraphrasing and summarising are important skills to practise because they are central to academic study. If you ignore these principles then you are plagiarising. It is often difficult to learn how to write in your own words, particularly if you think that the original source is so well worded that you could not possibly write as well yourself. There is also a temptation to cut and paste from resources in electronic form, because it is so easy to do. The following text has been copied and pasted directly from the Open University OpenLearn website in order to illustrate the process of paraphrasing, but we have been careful to attribute the source so that it is clear where it came from.

79

> ### *Try This*
>
> Read the following extract, then have a look at these examples of paraphrasing, and decide for yourself which is good practice. What are your reasons for deciding this?
>
> *Hangovers: Original Text*
>
> In certain cultures, an evening of heavy drinking is a regular social activity and the ill-effects suffered the following morning are accepted as an inevitable part of life. The economic cost of alcohol-related absence is frequently caused by workers experiencing symptoms of 'hangover'. This is the term used to describe the collection of symptoms that occur in drinkers on the day following a heavy drinking session, once the ethanol has been cleared from the blood. Even when a hangover is not severe enough to cause absence, it may severely impair the ability of a person to function effectively in the workplace. The economic impact of alcohol-related illness is dominated by these short-term productivity deficits, with chronic alcohol-related diseases only accounting for a small proportion of this cost.

The list below shows the most reported symptoms of hangover, with the commonest first:

- headache
- poor sense of well-being
- diarrhoea
- anorexia (lack of appetite)
- tremor (trembling hands) fatigue
- nausea.

Symptoms vary enormously between people and episodes, making research into this condition difficult, even without considering the ethical issues of deliberately making people ill. A variety of physiological mechanisms have been proposed that could reasonably explain the occurrence of hangovers, but without much evidence to back them up.

Source: Reproduced from unit SDK125_2: Alcohol and human health, from the online Open Educational Resource OpenLearn (http://openlearn.open.ac.uk/) reproduced with kind permission from The Open University.

Hangovers: Paraphrased version A

The term hangover describes a range of the symptoms which occur after heavy drinking. Although it is a part of the culture in some societies, it can create serious problems in the workplace leading to absences from work, or a reduced ability to complete the job properly. Hangovers may include a variety of symptoms, the most common being the headache and a general feeling of being unwell, although there is plenty of variation between individuals. It is not clear exactly what causes these symptoms.

Hangovers: Paraphrased version B

Hangover is the term used to describe the collection of symptoms that occur in drinkers on the day following a heavy drinking session. Alcohol related absence is frequently caused by hangovers, which may severely impair the ability of a person to function effectively in the workplace. The most reported symptoms of hangover are headache and a poor sense of well being, although symptoms vary enormously. The physiological mechanisms to explain the occurrence of hangovers are not clear.

Hangovers: Paraphrased version C

Hangovers are caused by heavy drinking the night before and may result in the following symptoms including headache, a poor sense of wellbeing, diarrhoea etc. Symptoms vary enormously between people and episodes. The physiological mechanisms are not clear.

Our comments on this exercise

This extract covers two areas: the symptoms of hangover and the economic impact, and so any effective paraphrase should cover both these areas. Version C only refers to the symptoms, and therefore is inadequate.

While Version B covers both major areas, it does so by copying out many of the sentences from the original and rearranging them, so it could be considered as plagiarism.

Version A is a more effective paraphrase because it covers both topics, and has been written in the author's own words.

However in the end the acceptability of these versions will depend on the course and level, so you would need to check with your tutor.

Quoting means selecting a sentence or short paragraph that someone else has written or spoken, which illustrates or encapsulates what you are trying to describe in your own written work. For example, sometimes the author might define terms or concepts which you wish to report exactly. You need to be wary of using too many quotes in your written work, because your tutor will be looking for evidence that you understand the issues. If your work consists of more quotes than your own words, he or she may assume that you do not understand what you are writing about. When using quotes you can cut and paste directly from the original source, but you need to make it clear which is the quote and which is your own work. You might put the quote on a new line, use italics or indent the quote like this extract:

As I was going up the stair

I met a man who wasn't there

He wasn't there again today

I wish, I wish he'd stay away.

Mearns, H. (1899)

Referencing is a way of providing the reader with enough information so that they can find the source which you were using. You must use a reference whenever you have drawn from someone else's work, and this helps the reader to distinguish between your own writing and what originates from someone else. A reference usually contains:

- the author(s) and title

- the name of the book or paper or site

- the publisher or a weblink

- the date of publication

- the date you accessed the link.

This tells you all you need to know in order to locate and read the resource for yourself: as we have done here for this excellent online tutorial.

> Place, E., Kendall, M., Hiom, D., Booth, H., Ayres, P., Manuel, A., Smith, P. (2006) *Internet Detective: Wise up to the Web*, 3rd edition, Intute Virtual Training Suite, [online]. Available from: http://www.vts.intute.ac.uk/detective/ (accessed 19 Mar 2009).

There are a number of different conventions and ways of recording references, and so we recommend that you find out from your tutor what is acceptable practice for your course and institution.

Your computer can help with effective paraphrasing, quoting and referencing. You might try cutting and pasting an extract of the original, and then making use of the highlighter in your word processor to mark passages or certain phrases of particular interest. You will then need to make brief notes of what the paper is about. It is a good idea to return to your notes after a day or so and then write an account in your own words. You might wish to illustrate your points with quotes from the original. You can also copy and paste the source into your bookmarking site or word-processed document so that you can find it again when you need it.

Quick tips: Using the information retrieved (word processor; social bookmarking)

- Learn to paraphrase, quote and reference appropriately:
- make sure you understand the meaning of the original source;
- note passages or odd phrases which are particularly important;
- make brief notes of the relevant areas in your word processor;
- bookmark or copy and paste the reference or link into a file of resources return to your notes and write them in your own words;
- include the paraphrase in your coursework;
- insert quotes to illustrate;
- include the reference.

FINAL COMMENTS

Plagiarism is a major problem in student coursework which you can avoid by developing sensible search strategies and in making appropriate use of the resources which you find. Finding good quality Internet resources can be time consuming. Perhaps the best way of finding information and resources that will help you with your study is to share your searching with others: this will also help you to build stronger social networks and shared communities of interest. We should not leave this chapter without stressing the importance of developing some scepticism in your approach to information which you retrieve on the web. Just do not believe everything you read. Having shown you how to collect some useful and relevant resources in preparation for coursework, the next chapter 'Writing and presenting' will discuss approaches to writing assignments.

10 Writing and Presenting

I think I'm beginning to get the hang of writing assignments for this course and it's really useful being able to use a computer for that. I make notes in a Word document, then cut and paste quotes. I find it a very creative way of doing things. I like being able to make one paragraph grow and another one shrink. You can't just stick something in the middle if you are working with paper copy.

As a student you are likely to be involved in a variety of writing tasks. Depending on your subject of study these tasks may include writing essays and reports, summarising and critiquing journal articles or book chapters, writing up lab reports or reflective diaries, and creating spreadsheets or graphs. You may well be expected to prepare oral presentations or seminar papers which will also require some written preparation. This chapter concentrates on the academic writing you will need to undertake as part of course assignments and it introduces examples of ways in which online and mobile technologies can help you.

85

ACADEMIC WRITING ONLINE

The use of technology has changed the ways in which we write, and provides new options and opportunities for constructing, editing and sharing written work. Not only is it easy to change your mind after the first draft and straightforward to store the file, but you can also use and re-version the same piece of writing for a variety of purposes over a period of time. So for example you might write some notes on course material and then add to them as your understanding grows. These notes can then become the basis of a formal assignment. Because of the connectivity of digital devices you might record audio or take pictures using your mobile phone which can then be used to illustrate your work. It becomes possible to download pictures or diagrams, or perhaps audio clips from the web and include them in your assignment, although you will need to clarify copyright and intellectual property rights (IPR) for each resource before doing this. By using an e-portfolio or web-based file-sharing tools your writing can be shared with colleagues who may comment or add to the document, perhaps as part of a collaborative project.

HOW ONLINE AND MOBILE TOOLS ARE USED FOR ASSIGNMENTS

Tools you might use

Word processor; spreadsheet; presentation software; audio recording; wiki; e-portfolio; file-sharing sites

The most well known and widely used suites of tools for writing are those which come as standard with all new desktop and laptop computers, or the freely available open source equivalents which can be downloaded from the Internet. Different variations of these software packages are available, but all of them include a *word processor* for creating documents, a *spreadsheet* tool for manipulating numerical data and *presentation software* for building slide shows. A growing number of options for creating and sharing different types of writing are also available online. One example of this is the *wiki* which has been specifically developed to encourage collaborative writing and is often in use for educational purposes.

Whatever the nature of your course you will certainly need to prepare written assignments. Assignments provide an important way for you and your tutor to check that you have a grasp of what the course was about. In some courses you may have to produce written work at regular intervals, whereas in others assignments come only at the end. The way in which you write and what you are required to write will depend on your course, institution and level of study. Whether your writing involves large amounts of text, or focuses more on numbers, diagrams or graphics will also be determined by your chosen field of study.

In many subject areas assignments take the form of word-processed essays or reports, and in some cases you may find that you are encouraged to illustrate these with photos, diagrams or graphs. Word processing your assignment can help you to write in clear and grammatical English using the spellchecker, grammar and word count tools. The structure of the document can be enhanced by adding or deleting text and moving paragraphs around, or by inserting tables, diagrams and graphics. Word processing can also help you to present work to its best advantage by formatting bold or italic fonts, indented text or even highlighting in a different colour. Most word-processing software also includes a range of pre-set styles and formats to suit different kinds of documents, from CVs to reports. Links to websites and online references can enliven the assignment, especially if the document is uploaded to the VLE and read online.

On some courses you might be encouraged to illustrate your assignment with data from a spreadsheet. Spreadsheets allow you to store, collate and manage numerical data, and report it in a variety of forms, including charts, summary tables and a variety of graphs. Spreadsheets have many sophisticated features including the ability to formulate all kinds of mathematical calculations, from basic to complex. The resultant tables, charts and graphs can be easily embedded within reports and presentations to highlight findings, make comparisons and illustrate trends (see Figure 10.1).

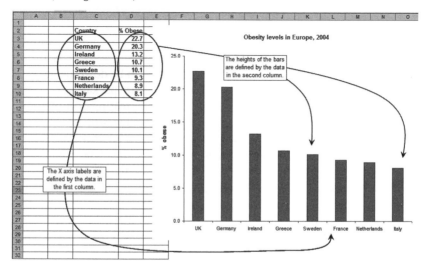

Figure 10.1   Use of a spreadsheet to create a simple bar chart

Source: Health status: indicators from the National Health Interview Surveys, European Commission: Eurostat, 2004.

Where coursework involves an oral presentation or poster then you may be required to make use of presentation software. This software allows you to develop an overall structure for your presentation in a series of screenshots or slides, illustrating your points with headings, text, pictures, graphs, web links or audio and video files. As with a word-processing tool, you can add, delete, and change the order of your presentation, supporting thought processes as you prepare your presentation. When used effectively, presentation software has the potential to enliven a presentation (particularly if you can use images, see Figure 10.2), and the next chapter provides some good practice guidelines for this.

Audio recordings can be inserted into the slide show. They are relatively easy to make either by using a mobile phone, a computer with

Perils of Online Study

Sometimes its easier to concentrate in a classroom

Figure 10.2   Use of presentation slides to illustrate a talk

microphone, or a digital recording device. The sound files could include a verbal explanation or conversation, or even some music or birdsong.

Sharing and collaborative writing

Some courses require students to give and receive feedback from fellow students. Files can be shared readily by attaching to an email, uploading to a VLE or a file-sharing site. The file can be returned with comments, using the reviewing option which allows readers to add comments and edit your document. You can then consider, accept or reject changes.

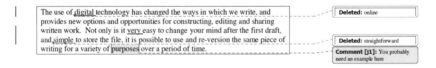

Figure 10.3   Use of reviewing tool in a word processed document

You may have access to a wiki, which provides a common area on the web or within the VLE where you can develop any work which requires editing or collaboration. A wiki is a web page which anyone can edit and is a powerful tool for collaborative writing. The wiki allows you to develop and edit a piece of work and return to previous versions if that is considered desirable, so nothing is lost. Fellow students can also edit the same page so that it is constantly updated. The software allows you to produce a series of linked pages, so that the work can be divided up and reorganised as it grows. It is also common to be able to see a history of who has edited the work and what changes they made. Some wikis allow you to subscribe, so that you can receive email updates on any alterations to the website as they occur, see Figure 10.4.

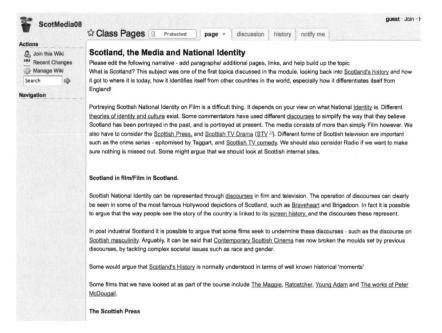

Figure 10.4   Use of a wiki for collaborative writing

Try This

Probably the most well known wiki at present is the online encyclopaedia *Wikipedia*, which has versions in many different languages. You might visit the site and explore the editing information that is available.

- Visit *Wikipedia* and select your preferred language.
- Click on one of the current items in the news on the home page.
- You will see that items in blue are linked to further pages in other parts of *Wikipedia*.
- To look at the changes which have taken place, click on the History tab at the top. Because *Wikipedia* has so many users, it changes all the time.
- You will see a list of revisions and you can see exactly what has changed when, and also compare different versions of the text.
- If you have a contribution to make on the subject you will first need to create an account.

http://www.wikipedia.org

(All web links are listed at the back of the book, and on our book website at: http://sites.google.com/site/learnonlinegroup/).

As an alternative to using a wiki, those who have an e-portfolio within the VLE can save their document there and give collaborators access to it. A public file-sharing site will do the same job. Both options ensure that the latest version of the file is always available to members of the group, where it can be edited and stored online for easy access.

OTHER FORMS OF WRITING FOR STUDY

We recognise that writing for course assignments is only part of the story. For example, you may be expected to communicate with fellow students and discuss the course concepts in online discussion forums: you can read about that in Chapter 6 on 'Communicating and community'. This kind of exchange can be helpful as a way of practice-writing the use of phrases and terms which are used as a part of the course.

Many students will also take notes in lectures and seminars, either as annotations on handouts provided by the tutor, or by taking a laptop to the lecture and using a word processor. These notes can be another useful way of practising writing within the discipline and can feed directly into the development of assignments when they come along. You can read a bit more about this in Chapter 4 on 'Listening, reading and sense-making'.

We referred briefly to the many resources on the web and the care which you need to take in accessing and using them. There is relevant material in Chapter 9 'Searching and researching' where you will find information about plagiarism and how to avoid it.

Finally, many courses still have a final exam which requires you to draw together what you have learnt on the course. Commonly you will be expected to write using pen and paper, which may come as something of a shock if you have become used to using your computer for all writing tasks, so do make sure you are prepared for this.

FINAL COMMENTS

Writing is central to study at university or college particularly because it is needed for preparing and producing assignments, whether they are written or oral presentations. A variety of online and mobile tools are in use for writing. Once writing is in digital form it can be readily edited, re-used and shared with others, and it becomes possible to integrate a variety of multimedia resources into written work. In the next chapter we will discuss how you might make best use of the technology to write well.

11 Writing and Presenting: A Survival Guide

...modern writing at its worst does not consist in picking out words for the sake of their meaning and inventing images in order to make the meaning clearer. It consists in gumming together long strips of words which have already been set in order by someone else, and making the results presentable by sheer humbug. The attraction of this way of writing is that it is easy.

Orwell, G. (1957, p. 150)

This comment did not come from a student. Instead it was written by the author George Orwell, some considerable time before computers were in regular use for writing. However it does illustrate how tempting it has always been to construct writing by using other people's words and to cut and paste from other sources, regardless of whether you are using scissors and glue or electronic means. Needless to say, this is not how you should approach academic writing or presenting!

Writing assignments or giving oral presentations at college or university is for many students a new and unfamiliar experience, and initially it can be rather daunting. However there are many ways in which online and mobile technologies can help you. In this chapter we suggest ways in which you might write for your course and prepare impressive assignments, while making effective use of your computer or mobile device.

WAYS OF WRITING

Writing has many characteristics; indeed what you write and the way in which you do it are all influenced by a number of factors. Here are a few:

Audience: who will read it? Is it someone you know? An expert or novice? An individual or a group?

Style: do you use full sentences? Abbreviations? Familiar tone or formal? Active or passive? First person or impersonal?

Length: a word; a sentence; a page?

Life: how long do you expect it to be useful for? An hour; a day; several weeks, or years?

Try This

Make a note for yourself of writing which you do regularly, and try to fill in this table with some examples.

Writing	Audience	Style	Length	Life
email	old friends	sometimes a bit boastful	two paras	two months
Job CV				
Article for school magazine				
Letter in birthday card				
Text messaging				
Reports for work				
Other?				

It probably comes as no surprise to you that writing for an academic course will be rather different to writing a job application or an article for the local newspaper. In fact, every discipline has its own particular approach to writing: so the way in which people write in history will be quite different to the way they might write in social care, or mathematics. Added to which, the expectations of your tutor will be different depending on the level of the course. The way in which these expectations are communicated to you may look foreign and unfamiliar too.

'I expect you to produce a coherent argument which includes a critical evaluation of the salient points of our discussion…'

GOOD PRACTICE GUIDELINES

Figure 11.1   What to write? Total confusion!

What do you do in order to survive all this? Before you write your first assignment or give your first presentation you need to have some idea of how to communicate effectively for the subject you have chosen to study, so the first job is to look for clues as to how to go about this. This is especially important at the start of a course when you might be feeling particularly lost in a fog of specialist terms and rather scary surroundings. One popular approach is to look for examples of written work which demonstrate how to write successfully for your course. That might be a piece of writing by another student, or perhaps examples of well-written material by a tutor. You might ask your tutor if they can give you examples to look at, or to discuss with your fellow students in an online forum. As Terry explains:

When I was starting, I was going into it blind, and model answers were a help, like: 'Oh yeah, I know where I'm going wrong'. Later in the course you can just get on and do it…

How We Learn 6

Every academic discipline has a distinct approach to communicating, which includes not only specialist terms, but also certain expectations of the appropriate way to communicate, and the correct way to write an essay or report. The distinct *academic literacy* of a discipline means that if you are new to a course you will need to learn appropriate ways to communicate, and you may have difficulty in getting to grips with the intended meaning of academic papers and other resources which you read. So it is not enough to learn 'how to communicate' at university, it is more likely to be helpful to learn 'how to communicate appropriately within the discipline'.

Source: Lea, M. and Street, B. (1998).

Ask your tutor to talk about assessment criteria and what they mean, and also to discuss the meaning of assignment feedback you have received. If you are communicating online this often works well on a discussion forum. For

93

instance if it is relevant you could try asking what 'critical evaluation' means and how one goes about critically evaluating anything. It is probably a good move to take every opportunity to attend tutorials and seminars if they are available, in order to learn about your tutor's approach to the course, and what forms of writing and other types of communication are acceptable.

Before exams come along there are similar issues in understanding how to write appropriately in a time limit, and finding out what the expectations are. You could try practising answers to past exam questions with fellow students. This can be done easily online, especially if you are able to find a good or not-so-good answer to compare your attempts with. Mary found this really helpful:

> Wow! I think this person comes from the 'write everything you know about' school of answering exam questions. They are wasting a lot of words and time putting in detail which would not gain any extra marks. I can see the time problem.

In the following section we give you some guidelines for writing assignments using a variety of tools.

ASSIGNMENT PREPARATION

Tools you might use

Word processor, presentation software, spreadsheet, audio recording and wiki.

Word processing offers a wide range of approaches to writing and presenting assignments, and enhanced possibilities for the redrafting of scripts. Assignment preparation involves several stages including:

- gathering relevant information;

- planning what to write;

- editing the written material;

- finalising layout and presentation.

Gathering relevant information

When gathering relevant information it is a good idea to practise reading purposefully, with the aim of looking for information to answer a particular question or to illustrate a point. You might use a forum to discuss your reading and to share resources with other students. You can type notes directly into a word-processed document or create a mind map of interrelated concepts as you study course materials or listen to a lecture.

By using cut and paste routines it is possible to transfer a piece of writing from one context to the next. In fact, the ease with which notes in electronic form can be cut and pasted means that they can be used directly as the basis for an assignment, but you should read the advice on plagiarism in Chapter 9 before you take this too literally.

Assignment planning and editing

People tend to plan less and revise more when word processing their work, and because it is so easy to edit the first draft does not need to be polished or even coherent. Indeed many people find that it helps to avoid 'writer's block' if they can get some writing done quickly, however rough and ready. So instead of detailed initial planning it is easier to produce a rough draft which can be edited gradually until it becomes coherent, and flows from one topic to the next.

To achieve this, it helps to write keywords in the margin of your printed draft or in a comments box within the document to describe the content of each paragraph. Having done this, you can then move the paragraphs around so that one paragraph leads into the next in a logical fashion. You then begin to draft sentences which join up the story from one paragraph so that it leads into the one which follows. This exercise also helps to show up areas which have been missed out, or to demonstrate where the same point has been covered in so much detail that it has used up the word limit and there is no room for writing on any other topic. If you are terrified that you might delete paragraphs which could come in useful later, it is quite comforting to maintain a 'cut-out' file, in which you save anything you have deleted from the main document: you can always retrieve that well-polished nugget of prose for use later.

The stages of gathering information, planning how to use it and editing the written version are closely interlinked and form an iterative process, which means that you will repeat them over and over until you have a result with which you are happy. But of course we are all different, and there is always plenty of variation in the degree to which each of us prefer to plan a structure before we start writing, or allow a structure to emerge as the writing progresses, or perhaps start to write the most familiar sections, leaving the tricky bits until last.

Word-processing software includes a range of features that help in checking your work, though they are never an alternative to proofreading it yourself. Some of the more commonly used ones are listed here.

Quick tips: word processing features for editing assignments	
spell checker	Highly recommended, particularly if your typing is less than perfect. Be aware that you can set the spelling for the country you are studying in: for example, English (UK) will be different to English (US). Be careful though because it is not able to distinguish between words which sound the same (to, too, two) so you need to be able to recognise the correct option.
grammar	Useful, particularly if you are not writing in your preferred language, but do not feel that you need to use all the suggestions which it offers.
word count	Invaluable for checking whether you are writing as much as you have been asked for. Tutors will often expect a note of the word count at the end of your assignment. Be aware that word counts do not always include text boxes.

Remember that an assignment that is well structured with an introduction, logically organised sections, a coherent conclusion and a full reference list is more likely to be well received by the tutor who marks it.

Quick tips: word processing assignments

- Cut and paste relevant sections from your notes into your assignments file;
- be sure to paraphrase the content of additional web resources or refer to them in quotes. Make sure that they are attributed (that means including details of the source) with the web link;
- name your files logically so that you can keep track of the latest version;
- remember to save your work regularly, every few minutes;
- read through your work to get an overview: you might find it helpful to print it at this stage;
- summarise what each paragraph is about: make a note in the margin;
- ensure that one paragraph flows into the next in a logical fashion;
- enhance your written work with illustrations or diagrams where appropriate;
- cut and paste references to any work which you have drawn upon, together with web links and the date when you last visited the site;
- be wary of fancy fonts or florid colours in your submissions. Your tutor will prefer a document that is well laid out, with generous margins and space between paragraphs and a font size of around 12 point;
- run a spell and grammar check;
- proofread your text with care;
- remember, it is the content of the assignment that will earn you the marks.

Assignment layout and presentation

The final stages of preparation involve layout and presentation, and it is likely that you will have guidance from your tutor on what is accepted practice. It is a good idea to allow generous margins using one or at most two simple fonts, and you may be encouraged to include pictures or charts. If you are publishing on the web, there is of course scope for including multimedia clips and live links to further resources. Indeed, once writing is in digital form it can readily be shared by email, or stored in a portfolio or file-sharing website for others to access.

ASSIGNMENTS WHICH INCLUDE SPREADSHEETS

Your tutor will probably provide some guidance on the format of your spreadsheet. You need to be aware of your prospective readers and ensure that you choose a layout which presents your data in the most accessible way. First you may need to decide whether a spreadsheet is appropriate, rather than a word-processed table. Then one of the most important aspects to get right is headings. Choosing meaningful headings for the rows and columns in your spreadsheet will help to make it understandable to others. This also means that if you create a chart or graph from your data it will have the right labels and definitions attached. Accuracy in data entry is vital as any errors at this stage will have a major impact on all your final calculations, so it is worth spending time double-checking to ensure that all details are correct.

Straightforward mathematical tasks such as addition, subtraction, multiplication and division are simple automated processes in a spreadsheet, but if you are required to perform more complex calculations many institutions provide training in spreadsheet use for students, so it is worth finding out what is available. As spreadsheets are in widespread use across business and education, you can also find freely available online training courses which can help, see Chapter 3.

Spreadsheets also offer a range of pre-set layouts and themes to suit different contexts, like word processing and slide presentation tools. Our advice is to keep it simple, and not to get seduced by an excess of colours or special effects. It is however worthwhile to familiarise yourself with the different graphs and charts which you can create with your data. Whether you choose a simple bar graph or pie chart or try out the more adventurous bubble or radar charts, the most important thing to remember is that it must present your data in the best possible way for your intended audience, and should not simply be a way to show off your spreadsheet design skills.

Quick tips: using spreadsheet data in assignments

- Choose your headings with care so that they make the data understandable;
- input data carefully and remember to check it;
- make use of formulae to perform simple calculations;
- choose an accessible layout which presents the data effectively;
- be wary of using too many colours and special effects in your graphs and charts.

DEVELOPING SLIDE PRESENTATIONS

Sometimes you may be required to give an oral presentation as part of your course, and it is useful to know how to develop slides to support this. Slides can be helpful in providing a framework for your thoughts, and for feeding into subsequent reports or essays. The process of developing slides demands that you think carefully about the framework of your message and the logical progression of ideas.

The slide presentation is generally projected on a screen from a computer, and it is common practice to produce handouts from the slides so that your audience can write notes as you make your presentation. For help with using the software we refer you to the online tutorials available from Open Office and Microsoft Office: see Chapter 3.

But before we go further, we would like to give you a list of our pet hates on slide presentations, speaking as long-suffering academic staff members who have sat in an audience through more presentations than are healthy for anyone.

Pet hates: slide presentations	Our comments
Lengthy text on each slide which presenter reads from	This can be very boring indeed
Lengthy text on slide, and you talk about something else	Which is more important: your voice or the screen?
Death by bullets	A killer
Visiting live websites during a presentation	This may add excitement but is often time wasting
Word art, gaudy colours and excessive animation	What do you want us to remember most about this presentation?

Starting at the beginning, your presentation should have a title, together with your name, details of the occasion and the date. Make sure that you use a consistent sans serif font throughout, preferably at least 30pt, with 48pt for headings, ensuring that the audience can read what you have written from the back of the room. You may decide to use one of the built-in style formats to provide a consistent look and feel for all your slides, or you can design your own. You will find lots of examples of the different styles others have used on file-sharing sites.

When constructing a presentation it is a good idea to use your slides as a way of providing an outline both for yourself and the audience. If you need prompts, then write yourself some notes for each slide. Think about the scope for illustrating what you have to say: you might consider showing photos, cartoons or diagrams. You might also embed audio clips to illustrate your points. The web has an extensive source of this material, but be aware that you always need to cite the source and take into account any copyright restrictions and IPR.

If you want to use the web during a presentation first check the availability of Internet access in the venue, then make sure that all links within your presentation are working properly when you get there. When using your browser, adjust the font size so that the website is legible from the back of the room, and check from the back of the room that you can read it. An easy and fail-safe alternative to visiting the web in a presentation is to take screen shots of the relevant pages and insert them into your presentation: the audience are unlikely to notice the difference.

Set your presentation to full screen and practise it beforehand, making sure that the slides are in logical order: you can expect to change them the first time you do this. It is also important to check how long it will take, particularly if your presentation is for an assignment where you need to be strict in your time keeping.

Finally, make sure that there is plenty of time in your presentation slot to allow for comments and questions from the floor. This is often the most important part of a presentation, when you learn how your written and spoken work is received by others. It can be an invaluable way of understanding the audience, particularly if you plan to write about the subject of your presentation afterwards and want to be sure that it is pitched to the right level and covers the right topics in appropriate detail. If you wish to share your presentation file with others after the event you can email it, make it available in your e-portfolio or on the VLE. To reach a wider audience, you can upload your presentation to a social networking or file-sharing site. We summarise here our favourite tips.

Quick tips: slide presentations

- Start with a title slide, with your name the title of your presentation and the date;
- use a sans serif font, at least 30pt with 48pt for headings;
- keep text on each slide to key points only;
- prefer meaningful graphics or diagrams to extensive bulleted points;
- allow one slide for about two minutes of talking;
- be sure to allow time for questions from the floor;
- practise your presentation beforehand, check it is visible from the back of the room and proceeds in a logical order;
- afterwards, share your presentation by saving it in your e-portfolio or a file-sharing site.

POSTER PRESENTATIONS

If you plan to give a poster presentation, then you will need to produce an attractive looking poster. The best way to do this is to design a single A4 page using your word processor or desktop publisher, and then go to a reprographics shop or print services within your institution and get it printed as A1 size. If you particularly wish to use colour you might find that it is more economical to use coloured pens after printing, since colour printing can be expensive. On your A4 sheet your body text should be set to around 12pt, with a title around 18pt. Your poster needs an informative but brief title, with your name and contact details if relevant. As for the main part of the poster, you might consider ways of summarising your topic with a diagram, picture or a few major points, just as we recommend for a slide presentation. There is a limit to which a potential audience will spend time in deciphering lengthy text in posters: most people prefer to listen to the author who can stand by the poster to inject some enthusiasm for the topic and summarise the important points. You might consider producing a few handouts which they can take away.

Quick tips: poster presentations (word processor)

- Design your poster as an A4 page, with text in 12pt and title in 18pt;
- use an informative and eye-catching title, include your name and contact details;
- summarise your project with a diagram, picture or few major points;
- print as A1;
- be prepared to stand by your poster and explain what your project was about;
- produce a handout for the audience to take away.

COLLABORATIVE WRITING

On some courses you may be required to write collaboratively with a group. The whole business of collaborating with fellow students can be strange and nerve-wracking, particularly if you are not familiar with the people you are working with. Just the act of changing someone else's work can seem rather ill mannered, and for that reason collaborative writing is often associated with an assignment, where each member of the group is required to undertake certain tasks within a given timeframe.

For collaborative writing there are various tools which you can use, notably the wiki which provides an online shared environment in which you can write, comment or amend the work of others. It can be a great way of writing together, while maintaining a copy of all amendments, so that you can always revert to a previous version if necessary.

Try This

If you would like to experiment with writing or editing a webpage, then you might wish to visit the website for this book. You may wish to explore, or edit what you find there.

http://sites.google.com/site/learnonlinegroup/

If you are required to contribute to a wiki, take every opportunity to meet regularly with your collaborators: the more you know the people you collaborate with, the easier it is to work with them. If it is difficult or impossible to meet face-to-face, then you need to devote some time to meeting online and sharing some information about all members of the group, so that you establish an online presence and feel you are part of a supportive community.

You will also need to discuss how you are going to work as a group. Divide up the jobs, for example share out different parts of the written work. Some individuals could be responsible for drafting, others for commenting, others for seeking relevant resources. You may need to decide what is acceptable practice in writing on the wiki: for example, whether each person will write in a separate sub-page of the wiki or on the same page; whether you want to include your name when you write a contribution, and if you are going to edit each other's work how much editing you will allow and in what timeframe you will accept edits. You also need to agree when you are going to access the wiki: it is common for only one person to be able to edit a wiki page at once, so if you are all trying to work on the last evening before submission, then you might encounter a few frustrated fellow students.

Quick tips: collaborative writing using a wiki

• Get to know the people you are collaborating with;
• decide who will undertake which task, whether writing, commenting, collecting resources;
• decide which part of the wiki group members will write to and whether they will have a page each;
• decide whether they should comment on, or edit each other's work, and at what stage;
• share timescales and study schedules to avoid frustration before assignment cut-off dates.

FINAL COMMENTS

While you may be anxious about writing assignments for a new course there are many well-tested approaches which can help, and a range of online and mobile technologies which can support the development of scholarly assignments. We cannot stress enough the importance of finding out how at the outset how to write appropriately for your course of study.

We started this last chapter with George Orwell and it seems appropriate to finish with him. He has the following rules for good practice in writing, and they are still good advice today.

Never use a metaphor, simile or other figure of speech which you are used to seeing in print.

Never use a long word where a short one will do.

If it is possible to cut out a word, always cut it out.

Never use the passive where you can use the active.

Orwell, G. (1957, p. 156)

Appendix A:
Web Links to Further Resources

A
AdAware: free anti-virus software
http://www.lavasoft.com/

Adobe Flash Player: free browser plug-in for playing Flash animations
http://www.adobe.com/products/flashplayer/

Adobe Reader: free download for reading Adobe PDF files
http://www.adobe.com/uk/products/reader/

Are you ready to study Science?
http://xww.open.ac.uk/science/courses-qualifications/are-you-ready-for-
    science/
then select Interactive Materials

Assistive technologies
http://www.gateway2at.eu/

Audacity: a freely available tool for recording and editing sounds
http://audacity.sourceforge.net

B
BBC computer tutor: use of mouse, keyboard and computer screen
http://www.bbc.co.uk/computertutor

Bebo: social networking site
http://www.bebo.com

Blogger: free blog tool
http://www.blogger.com

Bloglines: free web-based RSS Reader
http://www.bloglines.com/

British Library sound recordings collection
http://sounds.bl.uk

C
CiteULike: a free online service for managing and searching scholarly
references
http://www.citeulike.org/

Common Craft videos on social bookmarking, RSS, blogs and Twitter
http://www.commoncraft.com/blogs
http://www.commoncraft.com/twitter
http://www.commoncraft.com/rss_plain_english
http://www.commoncraft.com/bookmarking-plain-english

D
Daily Motion: a video-sharing website
http://www.dailymotion.com

Delicious: a social bookmarking site
http://delicious.com/

Digg: a social bookmarking site
http://digg.com/

Documentit: a tool for recording and managing citations
http://www.documentit.co.uk/

E
Elgg: a social networking site
http://elgg.org

Elluminate™ web conferencing
http://www.elluminate.com

F
Facebook: social networking site
http://www.Facebook.com

Flickr: file-sharing site for images
http://www.flickr.com

Freemind: open source mind mapping software
http://sourceforge.net

G

Get safe online: advice on safe computing: Search for peer-to-peer file
   sharing.
http://www.getsafeonline.org

Google: search engine
http://www.google.com

Google books: searchable books online
http://www.books.google.co.uk

Google Chrome: a free web browser
http://www.google.com/chrome

Google docs: a free web-based word processor, spreadsheet and file-sharing
   site
http://www.docs.google.com

Google maps
http://maps.google.co.uk/maps

Google Scholar: search engine for academic articles, journals and books
http://scholar.google.co.uk/

I

Intellectual Property Rights: a video about considering IPR when using
   Web2 resources
http://tinyurl.com/cngasv

Internet Detective: an online tutorial on searching
http://www.vts.intute.ac.uk/detective/

Internet Explorer: Microsoft's free web browser
http://www.microsoft.com/windows/internet-explorer/

iTunesU: audio files from universities around the world
http://www.iTunesU.com

L

Learn Direct: a range of online courses on using a computer
http://www.learndirect.co.uk/

M

Metacrawler: a search engine which gathers hits across several search
   engines
http://www.metacrawler.com

MindManager: concept mapping software
http://www.mindjet.com

Mozilla Firefox: free web browser
http://www.mozilla-europe.org/en/firefox/

N
National Archives
http://www.nationalarchives.gov.uk/cabinetpapers/

Ning: a social networking site
http://www.ning.com

O
Open 2.net: the learning portal of the BBC with the Open University (UK)
http://www.open2.net/learning/
then click on the Learning tab

OpenLearn: open content from Open University (UK) courses
http://www.open.ac.uk/openlearn.

OpenOffice: free office software suite for word processing, presentations,
    graphics, spreadsheets and databases
http://www.openoffice.org/
http://www.tutorialsforopenoffice.org

Opera: free web browser
http://www.opera.com/

Oxford Reference
http://www.oxfordreference.com

P
PB Works: a free publicly available wiki
http://pbworks.com

Plagiarism. Listen to students talking about plagiarism
http://www.heacademy.ac.uk/resources/ then search for student views
    plagiarism

Planet: the pdf user community
http://www.planetpdf.com

Q
Quicktime for Mac and PC: Apple software for listening to sounds and
    watching video
http://www.apple.com/uk/quicktime/

S

SAFARI: a guide from the OU on how to access, find and retrieve
   information
http://www.open.ac.uk/safari/

Safari web browser
http://www.apple.com/uk/safari

SCRAN database of culture and world heritage
http://www.scran.ac.uk

Second Life
http://secondlife.com

Skype
http://www.skype.com/intl/en-gb/

Slideshare: a publicly available file-sharing site which specialises in
   providing space for sharing presentations.
http://www.slideshare.net

Spybot
http://www.safer-networking.org/en/index.html

Study skills: advice from the Open University on studying, writing
   assignments and revising for exams
http://www.open.ac.uk/skillsforstudy/

Study Skills: a free resource from Palgrave to accompany their book
   series, usefully divided into discipline areas, and with accompanying
   podcasts
http://www.palgrave.com/skills4study/index.asp

T

Technorati: search engine for blogs
http://technorati.com/

Touchtyping practice
http://www.sense-lang.org/typing/

Tutorials: OpenOffice and Microsoft Office
http://www.tutorialsforopenoffice.org
http://www.homeandlearn.co.uk

Turnitin site
http://turnitin.com/static/popups/sample_report.html

U

UCAS: UK Universities and colleges admissions service
http://www.ucas.ac.uk

UK National Statistics
http://www.statistics.gov.uk/hub/

Using a computer for study
http://www.caledonian.ac.uk/student/ictskills/material/
http://www.open.ac.uk/pc4study

V

Virtual Training Suite: free Internet tutorials to help you develop Internet research skills for your university course
http://www.vts.intute.ac.uk/

Visible Body: a 3D interactive human anatomy model
http://www.visiblebody.com

W

Webguide: guide to using the Internet
http://www.open.ac.uk/webguide/

Wikipedia: online encyclopedia which can be edited by users
http://www.Wikipedia.org

Wikimedia: a suite of resources such as wiktionary and wikiquote which complement wikipedia
http://www.wikimedia.org

Windows Media for PC and Mac: Microsoft software for listening to sound or video
http://www.microsoft.com/windows/windowsmedia/default.mspx

Wordpress: a free blogging tool
http://wordpress.org/

Y

YouTube: video file-sharing
http://www.youtube.com

Appendix B: File Types and Common Web Link Codes

1. FILE TYPES

If you are to take full advantage of the many resources available, you will need to deal with a variety of different file types. The table below lists some of the most common file formats and explains the type of software and hardware tools you will need to use them. This is by no means a comprehensive list, but it does aim to highlight some of the most common digital formats you may come across when you are studying. You might want to make a note of those which are new to you so that you can do a bit of research to find out more about them and identify where you can get help to use them.

File names ending with-*	Type of file	Software/hardware/device needed
.doc	Microsoft Office Word document which can also include graphics, diagrams and special layouts.	PC or laptop with any version of Microsoft Office or Open Office installed. Can also be uploaded to, and opened in GoogleDocs if an Internet connection is available.
.docx	Microsoft Office Word 2007 document which can also include graphics, diagrams and special layouts.	PC or laptop with Microsoft Office XP or later, or Open Office installed. Can also be uploaded to, and opened in GoogleDocs if an Internet connection is available.
.rtf	Text document which can also include graphics, diagrams and special layouts.	Can be read with any word processing software.

File names ending with-*	Type of file	Software/hardware/device needed
.txt	Basic text document.	Can be read with any word-processing software, including Notepad which comes as standard with most PCs as does TextEdit on a Mac.
.pdf	A read-only document format.	Requires Acrobat Reader which can be downloaded freely from the Internet.
.ppt	A Microsoft PowerPoint presentation file.	Requires either the full version of PowerPoint which comes as standard with Microsoft Office or the free Open Office equivalent. The Powerpoint Reader tool allows read-only access to the file.
.pptx	A Microsoft PowerPoint 2007 presentation file.	Requires either the full version of Microsoft PowerPoint 2007 which comes as standard with Microsoft Office XP and above or the free Open Office equivalent. The Powerpoint Reader tool also allows read-only access to the file.
.xls	A Microsoft Excel spreadsheet file.	Requires either the full version of Microsoft Excel which comes as standard with Microsoft Office or the free Open Office equivalent.
.xlsx	A Microsoft Excel 2007 spreadsheet file.	Requires either the full version of Microsoft Excel 2007 which comes as standard with Microsoft Office XP and above or the free Open Office equivalent.
.mpg	A video file, usually also with sound.	To play this file you will need Windows Media Player or QuickTime, both of which can be download from the Internet for free. It can also be downloaded to MP4 players, newer iPods and some more recent mobile phones.
.wma	A windows media audio file.	This sound file can be played in Windows Media or QuickTime, both of which are freely available to download from the Internet.
.mp3 and .mp4	An audio file.	This sound file can be played in Windows Media or QuickTime, both of which are freely available to download from the Internet. It can also be downloaded to MP3 and MP4 players and all iPods, as well as audio-enabled mobile phones.

File names ending with-*	Type of file	Software/hardware/device needed
.exe	Files which execute a software programme.	These programme files work on their own simply by clicking on them and don't need any additional tools.
.gif or .jpg	Image files.	Can be opened with any graphics package. Free options such as GIMP are available to download from the web.
.htm or .html	A hypertext file.	Needs a browser such as Internet Explorer or Firefox to view.
.zip or .rar	A compressed file.	This needs a tool such as PKZip, WinZip or WinRar to unpack.
.wav, .avi or .mpeg	Video files.	These can be played in Windows Media or Quicktime.

* You can find a comprehensive list of file extensions at http://en.wikipedia.org/wiki/List_of_file_formats

2. COMMON CODES USED IN WEBLINKS

Type of organisation	
.ac or .edu	academic or educational
.co or .com	commercial
.gov	government
.org	non-governmental, non-profit making
.biz	business
.net	network or Internet-based services
.info	unrestricted use – 'information'
.aero	air transport industry
.coop	cooperatives
.mil	military

Country**	
.au	Australia
.de	Germany

Country**	
.fr	France
.it	Italy
.uk	United Kingdom
.us	United States
.es	Spain
.ie	Ireland
.in	India
.ru	Russia

** You can find a comprehensive list of country codes at http://en.wikipedia.org/
wiki/county_code_top-level_domain#List_of_ccTLDs

Appendix C: Glossary

aggregator	also referred to as a feed reader or news reader, this is an application which pulls together information from many different websites or blogs into one easily accessible digest
asynchronous	communication activities which do not require all participants to be online simultaneously, the most common example being online discussion forums which can be read and responded to at any time
audio blog	also known as an MP3 blog, this is a blog based on sound files rather than text, whose owner makes audio files available for others to download
audio over Internet	also known as Voice over Internet Protocol or VOIP, this refers to audio transmission (in this case voice) via the Internet
audiographics	a combination of digitised sound and images transmitted via the Internet
avatar	a personalised, three-dimensional character which represents your identity and which you control in computer games or in an immersive virtual world such as Second Life
Bebo	a well-known social networking site which is especially popular with younger users, whose title is apparently derived from the phrase 'Blog Early, Blog Often'
blended learning	commonly describes a combination of online learning and classroom-based learning, or specifically the use of virtual learning environments, discussion boards, blogs, wikis, audio conferencing and mobile devices alongside face-to-face lectures, seminars and tutorials
blog	short for web log, often used as a personal online reflective diary which can be commented on by others
broadband	often used as a generic term to describe a high-speed network through a cable which can carry multiple signals, and which provides much faster Internet access than a dial-up modem connection

concept map	a visual representation of a set of inter-related ideas, usually linked together with lines and arrows
de.licio.us	a popular, free, web-based social bookmarking site which allows the creation and sharing of lists of web links and resources
e-book	an electronic version of a book which can be read online or downloaded to a digital device
e-journal	an electronic version of a journal which can be read online or downloaded to a digital device
e-learning	the name often given to learning supported by technology
e-portfolio	a collection of web pages and digital resources created by the user to reflect their personal development as a learner or as a professional
EVS	an Electronic Voting System which allows individuals to respond to questions in lectures and seminars through the use of special handsets, with final results displayed as graphs and charts on a screen. Also known as Personal Response Systems (PRS) or 'clickers'
Facebook	a well-known social networking site which is especially popular with students
file-sharing site	specialist sites which allow the uploading and sharing of different types of files, including photos, images, slide shows, video and audio
firewall	software which prevents hacking, viruses and other malicious attacks on Internet-enabled devices and networks
forum	an online discussion board which supports text-based communication between two or more partipicants, normally organised in topic-focused discussions or 'threads'
Google	one of the most well-known search engines for finding information on the web, now also incorporating Google Scholar for searching academic articles, journals and books as well as Google Docs for creating and sharing documents online, Google Maps, Google Mail and several other useful tools
GPS	Global Positioning System, a satellite navigation device which helps you to identify precise locations
hand raising	a technique used to attract the attention of the Chair in an online conference session, for example by clicking on a particular icon, perhaps in the form of a raised hand, to denote that you would like to speak
HTTP	Hypertext Transfer Protocol denotes a set of processes used to transmit information over the web, commonly seen at the beginning of a web address

instant messaging	a form of communication which requires all participants to be present online at the same time to send and receive messages
iPod	a small electronic device developed by Apple primarily for storing and playing MP3 audio files: more recent versions can also be used for photos and MP4 video files
keylogger	a malicious device or software programme which can copy key strokes to identify passwords and other logon data
malicious software	a collective name for the various viruses, worms and trojans, also referred to as malware, which travel over the Internet and cause major damage to computer systems and networks
memory stick	a small storage device which plugs into your computer and can be easily carried around
Metacrawler	an overarching search engine which synthesises the results from several of the most popular search tools
metadata	information about a digital resource included in its source code which makes it easier to classify for storage purposes and to find in online searches
micro-blogging	a cut-down version of blogging which allows short messages to be distributed to a selected group of contacts by mobile phone texting, specific websites or instant messaging
mind map	another name for a concept map which is a visual representation of a set of inter-related ideas, usually linked together with lines and arrows
mobile device	a digital tool such as a laptop, mobile phone, MP3 player, e-book reader or Personal Digital Assistant (PDA) which can be easily carried around
MP3/4 player	a generic term for a portable electronic device which stores and plays MP3 audio and/or MP4 video files
MSN	originally the brand name of the Microsoft Network Services which included the Hotmail email service and the Messenger instant messaging tool, now re-branded as part of Microsoft's Windows Live suite. Despite this, the acronym MSN is still commonly used to refer to instant messaging services
MySpace	another well-known social networking site for communicating with friends, colleagues and family
open source	a method of developing software tools which allows them to be made publicly available at no, or minimal cost, with full access to the underlying source code to allow for further collaborative development and adaptation
operating system	software installed in every computer which is essential for managing its many functions including internal memory usage, disk space and file system
paraphrase	re-state an idea, topic or piece of text in your own words

115

personal development planning	an approach which encourages continuous reflection on experiences and progress, especially in a learning context, through collating either a paper-based or digital portfolio of evidence
plagiarism	copying the work of others without acknowledgement and passing it off as your own
podcast	a digital audio file which can be listened to online or downloaded to an MP3 player, audio-enabled phone or other personal device
polling	taking a vote on an issue, an activity which may be part of an online conferencing session, a lecture using an electronic voting system, or in an online survey
Powerpoint	a Microsoft product which allows the development of a set of digital slides which can contain text, graphics, audio, web links and animations, used to support talks and presentations
presentation software	a generic term for a software programme which allows you to create digital slides to support a verbal presentation
profile	a web page which provides personal information about an individual's background and experiences
PRS	an Personal Response System which allows individuals to respond to questions in lectures and seminars through the use of special handsets, with final results displayed as graphs and charts on a screen. Also known as Electronic Voting Systems (EVS) or 'clickers'
quiz	an online test which may include a range of question types such as: multiple choice; yes or no; drag and drop; matching pairs; and short text responses
quoting	taking a phrase, sentence or paragraph from a book or article and inserting into an essay, research article or report with the source appropriately referenced, to illustrate a point or provide supporting evidence
referencing	acknowledging the source of a publication or quote referred to within an essay, research article or report by providing full details of its author, date of publication, article or chapter title, book or journal title, and publisher using a standard referencing method
RSS	Really Simple Syndication, also referred to as a 'web feeds', is a means of disseminating newly updated information from web pages, blogs and wikis to interested subscribers who can read the short updates via a freely-available RSS reader
screen reader	a software tool which reads aloud text from a computer screen
search engine	a software tool for searching for information and resources on the web

Second Life	one well-known example of an immersive 3D virtual world
self-directed learning	learning in which the student takes the initiative to read or study as much as they need in order to meet goals which they have set themselves. Often used in the context of online learning, but sometimes it can be specific to informal learning, which takes place in every setting
server	a central computer which 'serves' other computers or 'clients' on a network by hosting shared resources and services such as email and file transfers
Skype	a popular software tool which enables free, computer-based Voice over Internet (VOIP) communication
Slideshare	a file-sharing site which allows the uploading and sharing of powerpoint presentations
smart phone	a mobile phone which also offers email, Internet access and other computing funtions
SMS	short message service, based on text messaging via a mobile phone or handheld device
social bookmarking	web-based software tools which allow the sharing of individual collections of web addresses and resources
social networking	websites which support networking activities amongst friends, families and colleagues in a branded environment through communication, file sharing and information exchange
social software	interactive websites which enable online file sharing and communication
spam	unsolicited junk emails
spell checker	a common feature within word-processing software which automatically highlights mis-spelled words and allows you to make corrections
spreadsheet	a software tool which allows the manipulation of numeric data
summarise	provide a short overview of the main points of a document, report, article, chapter or book
synchronous	online communication activities which take place in real time with all participants present, such as videoconferencing and instant messaging
tagging	a way of including key words or phrases in the metadata of a digital file or web page so that information about the resource can be easily found by search engines
TEL	Technology Enhanced Learning
Twitter	a popular software tool for micro-blogging

URL	Uniform Resource Locator, a unique address identifying web pages or other online resources
USB keylogger	a device attached to a computer which can copy key strokes to identify passwords and other logon data
vidcast	a combination of podcast (audio) and video streamed over the web or downloaded to a personal digital device
video conferencing	online simultaneous communication with two or more participants using both video and audio transmission
virtual world	often used to describe a simulated computer-based 3D environment in which it is possible for users to create 3D characters (avatars), artefacts and resources, interact with other participants and move freely within the virtual landscapes and buildings
virus protection	software which protects computer systems from attack by Internet viruses
VLE	Virtual Learning Environment. A piece of software which integrates a variety of online resources for learning such as discussion forums, quizzes, and instant chat as well as course information and content
voice-activated software	an computer application which can recognise and respond to a human voice
web 2.0	a generic term used to describe the second phase of web development which has moved from offering static information to creating dynamic and interactive tools for sharing, creating and communicating
web browser	a free software tool which allows you to access and interact with web pages and online resources
web chat	an text-based communication system which requires all participants to be online at the same time
web conferencing	a communication system which allows participants to meet online simultaneously and interact through audio, video, text and a shared whiteboard
web feed	also referred to as Really Simple Syndication (RSS), this is a means of disseminating newly updated information from web pages, blogs and wikis to interested subscribers who can read the short updates via a freely-available RSS reader
webcam	a type of digital camera attached to an Internet-connected computer or laptop which allows video connections between two or more participants
webcast	video and/or audio (podcast) files either streamed over the web or downloaded to a personal digital device

whiteboard	an synchronous online workspace which allows participants in a videoconference to share text, presentations, graphics, spreadsheets and web pages
wiki	a series of web pages which anyone can edit
wikipedia	a free online encyclopedia created using wiki tools which can be edited by anyone who accesses it
wireless network	a computer network which can be used without connecting cables by devices which are fitted with a wireless adaptor
word processor	software tool for creating, editing and managing documents

Appendix D: References

Jonassen, D. H. Davidson, M. Collins, M., Campbell, J. and Bannan Haag, B. (1995) Constructivism and computer-mediated communication in distance education. *American Journal of Distance Education* 9(2) pp. 7–26.

Lea, M. and Street, B. (1998) Student writing in Higher Education: An academic literacies approach. *Studies in Higher Education* 23 (2) pp. 157–172.

Marton, F. and Saljo, R. (1997) Approaches to learning. In: by F. Marton, D. Hounsell and N. Entwistle (eds) *The Experience of Learning.* (Edinburgh: Scottish Academic Press).

Meyer, J. H. F and Land, R. (2006) *Overcoming Barriers to Student Understanding: Threshold Concepts and Troublesome Knowledge.* (London: Routledge).

Orwell, G. (1957) Politics and the English language. In: G. Orwell *Inside the Whale and Other Essays.* (London: Penguin Books).

Pask, G. (1975) *Conversation, Cognition and Learning* (New York: Elsevier).

Perkins, D. (1999) The many faces of constructivism. *Educational Leadership* 57(3) pp. 6–11.

Perry, W. (1970) *Forms of Intellectual and Ethical Development in the College Years* (New York: Hold Rhinehart & Winston).

Place, E., Kendall, M., Hiom, D., Booth, H., Ayres, P., Manuel, A., Smith, P. (2006) *Internet Detective: Wise up to the Web*, 3rd edition, Intute Virtual Training Suite, [online]. Available from: http://www.vts.intute.ac.uk/detective/ (accessed 19 Mar 2009).

Säljo, R. (1979) *Learning in the Learner's Perspective. Some Commonsense Conceptions.* (Institute of Education Report, University of Gotingen).

Taylor, E., Morgan, A. R. and Gibbs, G. (1981) The orientations of Open University students to their studies. *Teaching at a Distance* 20 pp. 3–12.

Index